Gabriel N Cherish

Robert Burns
A Very Peculiar History™

With the Bard's own rhymes

'When Scotland forgets Burns,
history will forget Scotland.'

John Stuart Blackie
19th-century Scottish scholar

For Sheila and David Macdonald
'But pleasures are like poppies spread,
You seize the flow'r, its bloom is shed;
Or, like the snow-fall in the river,
A moment white, then melts forever.'

Robert Burns, 'Tam O' Shanter'
DS

Editor: Stephen Haynes
Editorial assistants: Rob Walker, Mark Williams
Illustrations: Jessica Palmer (cover), Mark Bergin,
Carolyn Franklin

Published in Great Britain in MMXII by
Book House, an imprint of
The Salariya Book Company Ltd
25 Marlborough Place, Brighton BN1 1UB
www.salariya.com
www.book-house.co.uk

HB ISBN-13: 978-1-908177-71-1

1 3 5 7 9 8 6 4 2

A CIP catalogue record for this book is available
from the British Library.
Printed and bound in Dubai.
Printed on paper from sustainable sources.

Visit our website at **www.book-house.co.uk**
or go to **www.salariya.com**
for **free** electronic versions of:
You Wouldn't Want to be an Egyptian Mummy!
You Wouldn't Want to be a Roman Gladiator!
You Wouldn't Want to be a Polar Explorer!
**You Wouldn't Want to sail on a 19th-Century
Whaling Ship!**

Robert Burns
A Very Peculiar History™

With the Bard's own rhymes

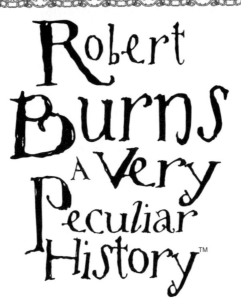

By **Fiona Macdonald**

Created and designed by **David Salariya**

'Sentimental doggerel'

Broadcaster Jeremy Paxman, 2009

'Uncommon invitin' in his speech...'

Farm girl Nelly Miller, c.1790

'Possessed in an extraordinary
degree the powers and failings
of genius.'

Edinburgh music publisher George
Thomson, 1796

'One of the great poets of the
human heart.'

Former Poet Laureate
Andrew Motion, 2009

Contents

Putting Burns on the map

Ayrshire

Greenock

Glasgow

A Y R S H I R E

Firth
of
Clyde

Arran

Irvine

Kilmarnock

Lochlie

Mossgiel

Mauchline

Ayr

Tarbolton

Alloway
(Robert Burns's
birthplace)

Mount Oliphant

Dalrymple

Maybole

Kirkoswald

C A R R I C K
(now part of
Ayrshire)

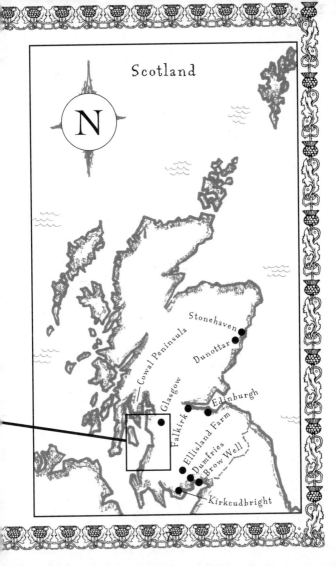

Mair nonsense has been
uttered in his [Burns's]
name – than in ony's barrin
liberty and Christ.

*from Hugh MacDiarmid, 'A Drunk Man
Looks at the Thistle', 1926*

Mair: more.   ony: any.   barrin: barring (except).

INTRODUCTION

Touching Scotland's soul

With MacDiarmid's words of warning (opposite) ringing in our ears, where do we begin? For almost 250 years, Burns has been a – no, *the* – Scottish cultural hero. A poet! A ploughman! A wild, natural genius! A studious book-lover! A loyal son, a loving father! A seducer, a libertine!

A carefree drunkard – or depressed and dyspeptic?[1] A celebrity, but with muddy boots and farmyard language that 'excites contempt by its meanness and uninteresting simplicity'.[2] A friend of nobles and the gentry. A fierce critic of pomp and privilege. A dutiful, tax-collecting, civil servant. A bold free spirit, champion of equality!

The man is a mass of contradictions. Indeed, we are so fascinated and perplexed by his short, intense, eventful life, that we often forget to read his poetry. In a 2004 Scottish survey, only 38% of men and 35% of women could recall a single verse from the works of 'The Bard'.

More recently, Burns has also been hailed as a friend of Scotland's Union with England – *and* as a supporter of Scots Independence. His name and image have been used – and abused – in every possible way, to promote 'Brand Scotland' all round the world.

---

1. *The latter. Burns frequently suffered from 'melancholia' – and terrible indigestion. As a remedy for the stomach trouble he ate home-made sheep's-milk cheese.*
2. Robert Heron, A Memoir of the Life of the Late Robert Burns, *1797.*

Countless things have been named after him, from an international humanitarian award to a diesel locomotive and (if campaigners have their way) an airport currently threatened with closure.

Burns has inspired films, festivals, musicals and, allegedly, Bob Dylan. There are karaoke versions of 'Auld Lang Syne'.[3] His works were sung and recited at the opening of the new Scottish Parliament in 2000; there were also proposals to give a committee room there his name. He is portrayed in over 200 grand public monuments, from the USA to China. According to the Scottish Government, 'The Kremlin Burns Supper is televised every year.' The same source[4] also confidently asserts: 'His is the voice of Scotland: "bold, Independent, unconquer'd and free".'

Whether that is true or not – and, remember, Scottish rebels had only recently been conquered by English-led armies at the time when Burns was born – it is what many people in Scotland and far beyond think and feel today.

3. which he popularised but didn't actually write; see page 179.
4. a speech by Scottish First Minister Alex Salmond, 2009.

The mere mention of Burns presses all the right buttons in many a Scottish (and other) breast to generate a warm, comforting, generous feeling of… what, precisely? Pride and patriotism – perhaps, but they are not the point. Much more important is a sense of recognition, understanding, shared humanity.

And that, whether you like Burns's poems or not, really is an astonishing achievement. Burns was born in poverty, suffered chronic ill health, had few opportunities and faced considerable misfortunes. Yet he created over 600 poems and songs that are still worth reading today, in spite of their sometimes obscure or difficult language. They are not all good: some are coarse and crude, some are sycophantic, some – yes, you are right, Jeremy Paxman (see page 4) – seem cloyingly sentimental. But the best will stand comparison with any other poems, from any place or any time. As Burns himself said:

My muse, tho' hamely in attire,
May touch the heart.

Bawdy Bard

In 1930, Scottish writer and feminist Catherine Carswell (1879–1946) wrote a pioneering, novel-like biography, *The Life of Robert Burns*, in which, for the first time in mainstream literature, she described several of the poet's love affairs, and quoted from some of his more lusty verses and boastfully explicit correspondence. Referring to all these, she remarked: 'Happily the time has come when the best minds can find nothing shocking in the frankness of the normal man which was so dear to the Bard.'

Alas, Carswell was far too optimistic. Soon after her book was published, she received a bullet through the post. With it was a letter suggesting that she kill herself, to leave the world 'a better and cleaner place'.

To lack sympathy with Burns is to lack sympathy with mankind.

Biographer Catherine Carswell, 1930

Readers, you have been warned. This is not a book for the 'primsie' (as Burns might have said), or for those easily offended by criticism of religious hypocrisy – or for the very young. But to discuss Burns's poems without reference to love – in all its forms – would be to misunderstand him completely:

> I never had the least thought or inclination of turning poet till I got heartily in love, and then Rhyme and Song were the spontaneous language of my heart.

Even so, you will find nothing here too coarse or outrageous – for that, you must read Burns's private letters, or leaf through *The Merry Muses of Caledonia* (c.1800), a collection of traditional bawdy ballads that Burns edited for his friends in the Crochallan Fencibles, an Edinburgh drinking club. Like any other writer – and Burns worked hard to turn himself into a serious author – he considered his audience, mostly removing obscenities from his own works or from old country songs before general publication.

14

A guid Scots tongue

Another word of warning. Burns spoke Scots – the traditional language of southern Scotland. And he wrote in Scots, as well as in English. Where we have quoted his Scots verses, we have added some words of English translation. Scots words used in the text are explained in the Glossary on pages 180–182.

Written down, Burns's texts can sometimes look rather forbidding. But, if you say the words aloud to yourself, or 'hear' them in your head (just like Burns did when he was composing), they will soon became familiar. So – read on, and enjoy!

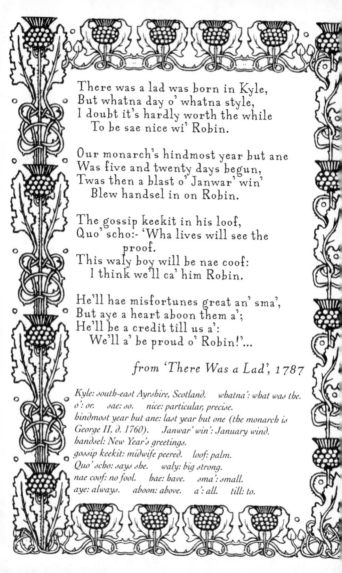

There was a lad was born in Kyle,
But whatna day o' whatna style,
I doubt it's hardly worth the while
    To be sae nice wi' Robin.

Our monarch's hindmost year but ane
Was five and twenty days begun,
'Twas then a blast o' Janwar' win'
    Blew handsel in on Robin.

The gossip keekit in his loof,
Quo' scho:- 'Wha lives will see the
      proof.
This waly boy will be nae coof:
    I think we'll ca' him Robin.

He'll hae misfortunes great an' sma',
But aye a heart aboon them a';
He'll be a credit till us a':
    We'll a' be proud o' Robin!'...

from 'There Was a Lad', 1787

*Kyle: south-east Ayrshire, Scotland.   whatna': what was the.
o': or.   sae: so.   nice: particular, precise.
hindmost year but ane: last year but one (the monarch is
George II, d. 1760).   Janwar' win': January wind.
handsel: New Year's greetings.
gossip keekit: midwife peered.   loof: palm.
Quo' scho: says she.   waly: big strong.
nae coof: no fool.   hae: have.   sma': small.
aye: always.   aboon: above.   a': all.   till: to.*

CHAPTER ONE

'THERE WAS A LAD'

At the height of his new-found fame, Burns felt confident enough to celebrate his own birth in the triumphant verses quoted opposite. He recalls a gossip's (midwife's) prophecy that, one day, he would make his family and friends proud. Later in the same poem, Burns also recalls the second half of the midwife's prediction: that he would have great success with 'the lasses'.

Whoever that old gossip was, she got things right all round. But Burns's verses also tell another true story concerning his birth.

Like the midwife's prediction, it seemed to foreshadow his extraordinary, turbulent future.

As Burns's poem says, he was born on 25 January 1759, during the darkest, dreichest season of the Scottish winter. He was the first child of a poor gardener and tenant farmer, William Burnes, and his wife, Agnes Broun. They lived at Alloway, a hamlet about 2 miles (3 km) from the town of Ayr in southwest Scotland.

As dusk fell on the 25th and a very pregnant Agnes took to the couple's best (and only) bed – it was a typical Scottish cottage box-bed, in the kitchen – a wild January storm raged outside the shutters. Desperate to get help for his new wife and his first child, now making its way into the world, Robert's father bravely ventured out into the howling gale, riding his horse through the treacherous, swirling waters of the local ford to fetch the nearest midwife.

In fact, mother and baby were both fine, but the weather remained frightful. After ten days, the little cottage, built by William's own hands, could withstand no more. In the dark hours before daybreak, with a sickening thud, one gable-end wall collapsed,[1] leaving baby Robert and his mother, and everything else in the kitchen, at the mercy of the savage storm.

Once again, William made a heroic dash through wild wind and driving rain, this time carrying his wife and child to safety with neighbours. The next day, determined that his home and family should survive, he returned to his storm-shattered cottage and patiently rebuilt it.

---

1. *The rain-soaked walls, made of clay, crumbled away from the waterproof stone-built chimney.*

No place like home

The cottage where Robert Burns was born still stands today. It is part of a large and glamorous new Burns Museum (opened in 2011), which, in the words of its own website, 'offers a truly unique encounter with Scotland's favourite son'. Attractions include:

- Burns Cottage, where Burns was born

- the ruined Alloway Auld (Old) Kirk, where Burns played as a child

- Brig O' Doon – the bridge over the River Doon that features in Burns's poem 'Tam O' Shanter'

- Poet's Path – a walk around Alloway, with works of art

- Burns Museum, home to the world's greatest collection of Burns manuscripts and artefacts

- the Burns Monument, erected in 1823.

Blowing up the Bard

In 1914, suffragette Fanny Parker and an unnamed accomplice tried to blow up Burns's cottage as a protest against the the British government's harsh treatment of campaigners for votes for women. They were chased away by the night watchman, who heard the noise of something heavy – canisters of gunpowder! – being moved outside. Parker was later caught and arrested. At her trial, she quoted Burns's famous lines:

Liberty's in every blow,
Let us do or die.

from 'Scots Wha Hae', 1793 (see pages 57–58)

Parker was found guilty and sent to prison, where she went on hunger strike. She was released ten days later.

Robert Burns's birthplace

21

That's no hovel ~
it's my home!

'About 50 years ago, the farm houses in the county of Ayr were despicable hovels; many of them were built in part, and some altogether, of turf, or of mud plastered on stakes and basket work.... That part of the building which served the family for lodging, sleeping, cookery, dairy &c... was about 12 or at most 14 feet [3.6–4.3 m] square, with the fire either in the centre, or in the gable, without jambs or smoke funnel. On larger farms, another apartment, of nearly the same dimensions... was called the spense, in which were stored the meal chest, sowen-tub, some beds, a cask into which the urine was collected,[2] known by the name of the wash-tub, spinning wheels and reel, when not used, and the goodwife's press, if she had one. The other part of the building was occupied by the cattle, which generally entered by the same door...'

William Aiton, General View of the Agriculture of the County of Ayr, *1811*

jambs: vertical supports either side of an opening.
spense: parlour, sitting room.   meal: ground oats, used to make
porridge and oatcakes, a poor family's main food.
sowen: oat bran (husks).   wash: liquid.
spinning wheels: simple hand- or foot-powered machines, used to spin
sheep's fleece into thread, ready to be woven or knitted.
press: store cupboard.

2. It was used to make vegetable dyes and to process woollen fabrics.

The parents of the Bard

If we knew nothing more about Robert
Burns's father, William, than his heroic efforts
to protect his wife and child from the
elements, it would be clear that he was a
remarkable man: resourceful, determined,
hard-working and devoted to his family. But
there is more:

William Burness was born in 1721, at
Dunottar near Stonehaven in the north-east of
Scotland.[3] He was the son of a well-educated
but extremely poor tenant farmer. Like his
father, he shared a thirst for knowledge and a
love of reading. But times were hard (see page
31), and by the late 1740s, William's father
could no longer afford to pay the rent for
his miserable smallholding. Young William
and his brother Robert were forced to leave
home. In 1848, William walked the 112 miles
(180 km) south to Edinburgh, Scotland's
capital, where he found work as a gardener.

3. See the map on page 7.

23

One 's' or two?

For generations, the Burns family had spelled their name 'Burnes' or 'Burness'. William kept to those spellings all his life, but his sons, including Robert, changed to the shorter, simpler 'Burns'. This form was more common – and more acceptable – in southwest Scotland, where they were born.

After two years William left the big city to work for wealthy landowners in Ayrshire. He did well, and was respected, but he longed to be independent. By 1756 he had saved enough to rent a small plot of land at Alloway, where he planned to set up a market garden. The same year, still a bachelor at 36, he fell in love.

His sweetheart was Agnes Broun, and she was 12 years younger. They met at the annual fair in the nearby village of Maybole. Agnes's family lived on the Carrick coast of Ayrshire; they made a (fairly) good living as part-time smugglers. Agnes's early life had been hard; when just 10 years old, she had cared for five brothers and sisters after their mother died. Now she lived with her grandmother and an old, blind uncle.

Agnes Broun was quick, neat and clever, busy and cheerful; later, one of her daughters described her judgement as 'uncommonly sound and good'. She was skilled at work around the home and on the farm, cooking, cleaning, spinning thread, helping with the harvest and caring for livestock. She loved to sing – she had a fine voice. People said she was pretty. She had red hair, rosy cheeks, and intense, deep brown eyes framed by dark, brooding brows. Robert Burns inherited these last two features.

William built his house, and wed Agnes in 1757. They kept three cows – Agnes made cream cheese to sell – but William went on working as a gardener. Within 20 months of Robert's birth, another son, Gilbert, arrived. By the time Robert was 12, he had been joined around the Burns family hearth by six little brothers and sisters.

Robert Burns's parents and siblings

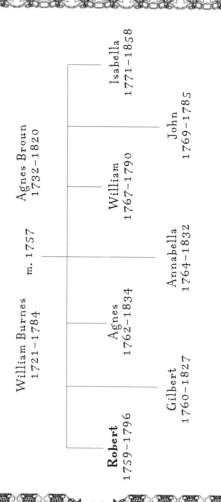

William Burnes
1721–1784

m. 1757

Agnes Broun
1732–1820

Robert
1759–1796

Gilbert
1760–1827

Agnes
1762–1834

Annabella
1764–1832

William
1767–1790

John
1769–1785

Isabella
1771–1858

Home, sweet home

Looking back, Robert Burns painted a sentimental picture of a poor but happy family — just like his father's:

...November chill blaws loud wi' angry sugh;
The short'ning winter day is near a close;
The miry beasts retreating frae the pleugh;
The toil-worn cottar frae his labour goes —
This night his weekly moil is at an end,
Collects his spades, his mattocks and his hoes,
Hoping the morn in ease and rest to spend,
And weary, o'er the moor, his course does
      hameward bend.

At length his lonely cot appears in view,
Beneath the shelter of an aged tree;
Th'expectant wee-things, toddlin, stacher
      through
To meet their dad, with flichtering noise and
      glee.
His wee bit ingle, blinking bonilie,
His clean hearth-stane, his thrify wifie's smile,
The lisping infant, prattling on his knee,
Does all his weary carking cares beguile.

blaws: blows.   sugh: sigh.   miry: muddy.   frae: from.
pleugh: plough.   hameward: homeward.

stacher: stagger.   flichtering: flittering, restless.
wee bit ingle: small fire.   stane: stone.   carking: worrying.

Belyve, the elder bairns come drapping in,
At service out, amang the farmers roun';
Some ca' the pleugh, some herd, some tentie
      run
A cannie errand to a neighbour town:
Their eldest hope, their Jenny, woman grown,
In youthful bloom, love sparkling in her e'e,
Comes hame; perhaps to show a braw new gown
Or deposit her sair-won penny-fee,
To help her parents dear, if they in hardship be.

With joy unfeigned, brothers and sisters meet
And each for other's welfare kindly spiers;
The social hours, swift-wing'd, unnotic'd fleet;
Each tells the uncos that he sees or hears.
The parents partial eye their hopeful years;
Anticipation forward points the view;
The mother with her needle and her shears,
Gars auld claes look amaist as weel's the new;
The father mixes a' with admonition due....

from 'The Cottar's Saturday Night', 1785

belyve: by and by.   bairns: children.   amang: among.
ca' the plough: follow the plough (are ploughmen).
tentie: carefully.   cannie: wise, cautious, prudent.   e'e: eye.
braw: fine.   sair-won: hard-earned.

spiers: asks, enquires.   uncos: news (i.e. unusual or uncommon events).
partial: lovingly prejudiced towards them.   gars: makes.
claes: clothes.   amaist: almost.   as weel's: as well as.   a': all.

from dream to nightmare

In 1766, when Robert was 7 years old, William Burnes began to live his dream: a farm of his own. It was on poor, bleak, treeless, stony land, at Mount Oliphant south of Alloway, and the rent was expensive.

William planned to sell the Alloway cottage to pay for seeds, livestock and simple farm machines – a wooden plough, hand-held spades and flails. There was a small, damp, stone-built house; William planted fruit trees and took with him two horses, several chickens and ducks, and Agnes's cows.

Before long, the whole family realised that William had made – as he himself admitted – a 'ruinous bargain'. The dream was becoming a nightmare. He could not find a buyer for the Alloway cottage, and, even with a hard-working wife and willing young sons to help him, it was almost impossible to make a living on a small, 'unimproved' (see pages 32–35) rented farm. The Burnes family often went hungry, and young Robert's physique was permanently weakened by 'unceasing moil'[4] in all weathers. But together, the Burnes family struggled on for 11 years, until their lease ended and they were free to leave.

4. *backbreaking physical labour – by the time Robert was 10, he was ploughing and helping with the threshing.*

Scotland – a poor relation?

Robert was born in 1759, just 13 years after Scottish Jacobites[5] (brave, romantic, patriotic, but a minority) had been defeated[6] by troops loyal to the Hanoverian dynasty who ruled from London. After this failed rebellion, Scotland was still under something of a cloud – politically, socially and economically. Even before this upheaval, when compared with richer, more industrialised, England, the whole of Scotland was very, very poor.

5. *supporters of the exiled survivors of the Stuart dynasty.*
6. *at Culloden, near Inverness, in 1746.*

The old ways

When Robert Burns was a child, many Scottish Lowland farms were still 'unimproved'.[7] The land was divided into narrow 'rigs' (ridges), separated by boggy drainage ditches. It was worked by the whole community.[8] The best, 'inbye', land, close to the village, was planted with the same crops year after year; the soil soon became exhausted. Poorer land, the 'outbye', was occasionally ploughed; but generally it was used for grazing cattle.

The richest, most fertile soil, beside rivers and lochs, was often too marshy for farming – but it did breed disease-carrying mosquitoes. There were no hedges and few walls to protect crops from straying animals. Big trees, which might have sheltered land from winter winds, had mostly been cut down for building or firewood.

7. *Landscape and climate made farming in the Scottish Highlands just as difficult but rather different.*
8. *Legally, the land was owned by rich noble families, but traditional 'townships' (village communities) had ancient rights to occupy it.*

Ignorance and poverty

Old Scottish breeds of sheep, cattle and horses were hardy, but small, tough and scrawny. The main Scottish crops – oats and barley – gave poor yields. In rainy summers, the hay harvest was a washout.

Some farmers did not know how to rotate (change) crops to avoid pests and diseases, or how to leave good land fallow to recover, or how to spread lime and manure to improve soil fertility. Others were simply too poor or exhausted to make any improvements.

The 'improvers'

But, throughout the Lowlands, enterprising Scots were busy doing just that. Advised by experts from the Netherlands, Scandinavia and England, they drained marshes, planted hedges, built walls, roads and bridges, spread lime and manure, planned three- and four-year crop rotations, tilled the land with new, faster, horse-drawn ploughs, bred improved varieties of grain, sheep and cattle, and sowed new seeds, such as flax, clover and turnips.

Keen to make a profit, landowners also let small farms to new tenants. Like William Burnes, these were often 'strangers' from outside old village communities. William and his sons had heard of the latest improvements and were keen to try them. But rents were rising faster than farm-produce prices. Without money to buy fancy seeds and lime, or employ tree-planters and ditch-diggers, they could only make slow progress.

The constant struggle of poor farmers to survive formed the background to Burns's poems, along with a strong sense of injustice, frustration, missed opportunities, and, often, utter physical exhaustion:

> For though I be poor, unnoticed, obscure,
> My stomach's as proud as them a', man.

Looking back in 1787, Burns wrote:

'We lived very poorly....A novel-writer might perhaps have viewed these scenes with some satisfaction, but so did not I; my indignation yet boils at the recollection of the scoundrel tyrant's[9] threatening epistles, which used to set us all in tears.'

9. the landlord's factor (business manager), who wrote letters threatening eviction when William Burnes was unable to pay the rent.

Some Lowland farming 'improvements'

1698 Politician Andrew Fletcher of Saltoun (1655–1716) is concerned by the 'abject and miserable' condition of Scotland's countryfolk.

1700–1750 Landowners introduce new breeds of sheep from the Borders and England.

1707 Union of Scotland with England opens new markets south of the border, especially for Scottish beef and wool.

1723 Scottish Society of Improvers in the Knowledge of Agriculture founded.

1725 Turnips first planted on a large scale in Scotland, to provide winter fodder for cattle.

1734 Potatoes grown on a large scale.

1735 The 'Ormiston Turnip' (34 lb/15.4 kg) goes on display in Edinburgh. Landowner John Cockburn builds a 'planned village' for farm workers and pioneers improvements in malting, milling and linen production.

1736 Landowners, scientists and scholars join Ormiston Society to discuss new developments in agriculture.

1760–1830 Lowland Clearances: tens of thousands of poor country people are forced by landlords, or by poverty, to leave their cottages and fields. Some find work in growing cities, others emigrate.

1763 James Small of Berwickshire invents Scots Plough, with cast-iron share (blade). This puts less strain on ploughmen and their horses.

1772 Andrew Meikle (1719–1811) invents safer, more easily controlled 'spring sails' for windmills (used to grind grain).

1778 Andrew Wright publishes *The Present State of Husbandry in Scotland* to advise livestock farmers.

c.1785 By now, around 150,000 Scottish cattle are sold at each Falkirk tryst (a cattle fair held once a month, August to October).

1786 Andrew Meikle invents first effective machine to thresh corn (separate the grains from the stalks).

1790 Forth–Clyde Canal improves transport of farm produce and other bulky goods.

1791 *Statistical Account of Scotland* reviews Scotland's geography and land-use; its aim is 'national improvement'.

1789 William Halbert publishes *The Practical Figurer or An Improved System of Arithmetic* to help farmers, surveyors and engineers make accurate calculations.

My father was a farmer upon the
    Carrick border, O,
And carefully he bred me, in decency
    and order, O,
He bade me act a manly part, though I
    had ne'r a farthing, O,
For without an honest, manly heart no
    man was worth regarding, O....

from 'My Father Was a Farmer', 1782

bred me: brought me up.
farthing: the smallest British coin, worth one quarter of an
old penny.

CHAPTER TWO

'IN YOUTHFUL BLOOM'

In 1787, when a young, handsome, unknown and thrillingly unpolished farmhand poet was, for a while, the toast of fashionable Edinburgh, admirers praised 'the heaven-taught ploughman' for his genius. Robert Burns – for it was he, of course – enjoyed the adulation.

But it also made him uneasy. Although only 27 years old, he had already experienced enough of the ups and downs of life (mostly the downs) to understand that fortune was fickle. Soon, he knew, the gentlemen of Edinburgh would open their doors to new favourites;

soon, the elegant ladies of Scotland's capital would welcome the next sensational visitor to their drawing-rooms.

There was another reason why the praises heaped on Burns made him uncomfortable: they were not true. Yes, he might thank God[1] for his lively intelligence, excellent memory, and powers of observation. But all the rest – his way with words, his skill with rhymes, his clever choice of rhythms and metres – were not a casual, random gift from on high. Rather, they were the result of painstaking private study, careful teaching, and years of practice. So were Burns's knowledge of four different languages (Scots, English, French and Latin), his skill at letter-writing, and his vast repertoire of traditional stories, myths and legends.

1. Today, Burns would probably call himself an agnostic. He held Christian beliefs as a child, but lost them as he grew older, though he continued to admire Jesus as the 'amiablest of characters'.

Less inspiration, more perspiration

'I have not a doubt but the knack, the aptitude, to learn the muses' trade, is a gift bestowed by Him "who forms the secret bias of the soul"; but I as firmly believe that 'excellence' in the profession is the fruit of industry, labour, attention, and pains.'

from a letter written by Burns, 1789

An 'improving' education

So, if 'heaven' did not teach Robert Burns, who did? First and foremost, his father. Almost as soon as he became a parent, William Burnes devoted his scarce leisure time to writing a 'Manual of Religious Belief' for his sons and daughters. He told them stories of his early life and ambitions. Together with Agnes, he taught them all he knew about farming.

The sound of music

What with seven children, helpers on the farm and occasional long-stay visitors, the Burnes's cottage was always full of 'crack' (conversation) and music. Agnes sang as she went about her work; Robert's sisters were also good singers. Their choice was traditional but far from polite; favourites included saucy love-lyrics and bawdy ballads:

> O John, come kiss me now, now, now!
> O John, my love, come kiss me now!
> O John, come kiss me by and by,
> For weel ye ken the way to woo!…

weel ye ken: you know very well.
woo: make love.

Young Robert loved music and dancing, and learned the words of all his mother's songs. These lyrics belonged to ordinary people, like the Burnes family and their friends. They were part of Scotland's history.

However, strangely, for a boy who grew up to become one of the world's best-ever songwriters, Robert could not sing a note in tune. He said he could hear the music in his head, but all he could do was hum it to himself, very quietly.

Wild fantastic!

Young Robert also loved to listen to stories told by Betty Davidson, an elderly cousin who often visited the Burnes family. This old lady's memory was a treasure-house of traditional tales, the more outlandish and extraordinary, the better. On dark winter evenings she sat in the firelight with the Burns children at her feet, telling them of the ghosts that danced in the ruined church at Alloway, the lost souls that howled in the wind and the rain, the fairies that lived under green grassy hills, the witches and warlocks that might drive their horses mad, and the sharp-fanged, burning-eyed monsters that lurked in the shadows of their very own stackyard.[2]

Later, Robert admitted that Betty was 'remarkable for her ignorance, credulity and superstition'. But even so, as he wandered over the moors after dark (he became very fond of midnight rambles) he could not help himself keeping 'a sharp look-out in suspicious places', just in case one of Betty's ghosts or monsters was still lingering there.

2. a yard where stacks of hay or grain were kept.

feeding the mind

Pious, serious, practical William Burnes had no time for such fairytale nonsense. However, like his own father, he had ambitions for his children. His family might be poor, his boys and girls might go barefoot, and their clothes were undoubtedly shabby, but their minds were just as good as any young lord's. As his son Robert later put it:

> Rusticity's ungainly form
> May cloud the highest mind...

William did not want his children to waste their talents in a dour struggle for survival. As poor tenant farmers, their lives could easily have been little better than that of the animals they cared for. But he wanted them to grow, spiritually, intellectually.

William Burnes was not alone in his appreciation of the opportunities a good education might bring. In advance of its richer neighbour England, poor, 'primitive' Scotland had provided basic state schooling, through the Kirk (see page 44), since 1560. This meant that even the poorest Scots could read, and knew something of history, geography and the Bible – as well as taking a lively interest in politics. The parish schools were open to all youngsters, though the quality of instruction varied. As soon as possible (before Robert was 6) William Burnes sent his children to the local school, 2 miles (3.2 km) away, at Alloway Mill.

Learning at home

In 1765, the parish schoolmaster left Alloway Mill. So, with four neighbouring families, William Burnes filled the educational gap by setting up an 'adventure'[3] school for local children. Arrangements were simple; parents hired a *dominie* (teacher), a keen local 18-year-old, John Murdoch. In return for the lessons he gave, he was provided with food and lodgings in his pupils' homes, and received a small salary.

3. *privately funded.*

The power of the Kirk

In Lowland Scotland, and parts of the Highlands, the Kirk (Church of Scotland) had tremendous authority. Founded in 1560, when Scottish Protestants broke away from the Catholic Church in Rome, its mission was to 'bring the ordinances of religion to the people of every parish in Scotland'. To achieve this, Kirk leaders – lay elders and ordained Ministers – compelled attendance at Sunday services, and held religious courts, known as Kirk Sessions, to enforce strict moral standards. From its beginnings, the Kirk encouraged education, so that everyone would be able to read the Bible.

In 1697, many believers had been appalled when the Kirk successfully encouraged a Scottish state court to hang 18-year-old Tom Aikenhead for blasphemy. (Tom, a student, had said he did not believe in the supernatural teachings of the Bible.) By Robert Burns's day, 60 years later, Kirk leaders were divided between strict, tough 'Old Lichts'[4] and more relaxed 'New Lichts' (moderates).

4. Licht *is a Scots form of* light.

Young though he was, Murdoch tried hard. He taught his pupils the subjects he knew best: English grammar, spelling and composition, the classics of English literature (he once frightened the younger Burnes children by reading a particularly gruesome passage from a Shakespeare tragedy to them), and the Psalms of David from the Bible.

Murdoch stayed in Alloway for about two years, until 1772. Robert was not yet 8 years old; but it was the end of the longest uninterrupted period of education he ever received. By the time they were 9, most children from poor families were sent away to earn their keep, as servants in a big house or workers on a farm. But, as Robert remembered, it was his father's 'dearest wish and prayer to have his children under his own eye till they could discern between good and evil'.

Scots mither tongue

By the 1750s most Lowland Scots, young Robert Burns included, were taught to read and write English. But this was not their first language – that was Scots, the 'mither tongue' they spoke and sang at home.

Scots was related to, but separate from, the English spoken south of the Border. A mixture of Old English, French, Dutch and Middle Low German, it also had words borrowed from Gaelic (from the Scottish Highlands and Islands), Latin, and Scandinavian languages.

From around 1400, Scots became a 'prestige' tongue, spoken by royalty – including the glamorous Mary, Queen of Scots – nobles and Church leaders. It was also the language of the independent Scottish Parliament, until that was suspended, after the Union with England, in 1707.

From then on, Scots fell rapidly out of favour. Powerful Scottish people headed south – and learned English, so they would be understood there. In 1761, just two years after Robert Burns was born, an Englishman opened elocution classes in Edinburgh. Before long, a group of Edinburgh citizens set up a 'Society for Promoting the Reading and Speaking of the English Language in Scotland'.

Robert and his brothers and sisters were all expected to help on the family farm. But William Burnes did not neglect their education. After farm chores were done, he continued their lessons himself, in English and religious studies. He borrowed books from the local Kirk Minister and the Ayr Book Society.[5] All were solemn and ponderous, on topics such as Sin, Death and Bible History, but Robert read them all.

In 1772, William sent Robert, now 13, and his younger brother Gilbert to school in Dalrymple, about 3 miles (5 km) away, to improve their handwriting.[6] William could not afford to send both boys to Dalrymple, and he needed their help at home. So Robert and Gilbert shared a place in the handwriting class, taking turns to spend two weeks at school followed by two weeks working on the farm.

5. *As with public schooling, Scotland was a pioneer. Book societies (early lending libraries) played a vital part in helping poor people to learn and increase their opportunities. The first public library in Scotland was set up in Innerpeffray, Perthshire, in 1680 by Lord Madertie.*
6. *This was not as frivolous as it might sound. In an age before typewriters and computers, neat, quick, regular, legible writing, together with perfect spelling, were essential skills for any ambitious young man hoping to escape from the drudgery of farm work to a better-paid, higher-status clerical job.*

The following year, 1773, William sent Robert to stay with John Murdoch, who was now teaching at Ayr. He wanted Robert to start lessons in French and Latin. For the first time, Robert mixed with pupils from better-off families; he found that he was just as clever – and twice as quick-witted. He discovered, too, that they shared his love for jokes and stories. For most of the time (except when siezed by sudden deep depressions)[7] the rough lad from out of town was good fun.

At Ayr, Robert borrowed books on geography, history and science from Murdoch and his friends. Not long after, Robert's uncle purchased (by mistake) a guide to writing elegant letters. It seemed hardly relevant to Robert's muddy life on the farm, but, like any other book he could get his hands on, he studied it eagerly.[8]

7. Some biographers have suggested that Burns suffered from bipolar disorder; certainly Burns himself described spells of 'hypochondria', 'melancholia' and 'blue devils', and also times of wild elation. Others have suggested that, while Burns was a man of deep – and very volatile – feelings, we should not confuse his writer's gift for describing them vividly with symptoms of actual illness.

8. As an adult, Burns was a keen member of Kircudbright Subscription Library, and always kept a wooden box of books in the parlour, ready to read at any time.

Practice makes perfect

Although he had no-one to write to, Robert loved to compose letters in all the different styles suggested by his uncle's book. He wrote just for fun, but his efforts revealed an unexpected talent: he could use words convincingly in any way he chose.

In 1775, when Robert was 16, his father sent him away again, this time to Kirkoswald.[9] A master there taught practical mathematics to boys from farming families. At first, as Robert remembered, he made 'pretty good progress', but then, for the first time – although most definitely not the last – his mind was distracted from the task before him by a charming young woman.

A new chapter in his life was opening…

9. *about 10 miles (16km) from home.*

...But first and foremost, I should tell,
Amaist as soon as I could spell,
I to the crambo-jingle fell;
   Though rude and rough –
Yet crooning to a body's sel,
   Does weel enough.

I am nae poet, in a sense:
But just a rhymer like by chance,
An' hae to learning nae pretence:
   Yet, what the matter?
Whene'er my Muse does on me glance,
   I jingle at her...

'Epistle to J. Lapraik', 1785

amaist: almost.   *crambo: puzzle or game.*
jingle: poem or song.   *a body: a person.*   *sel: self.*
weel: well.   *nae: no.*   *hae: have.*

In the second verse quoted here, Burns
is playing a game with his readers. He
knows, and he knows we know, that
only a man who has learnt something
about ancient Greek and Roman culture
would – or could – write about a Muse
(a goddess who inspires).

CHAPTER THREE

'Of
INDEPENDENT
MIND'

I t is sometimes said that teenage troubles were not invented until the 1950s. Young Robert Burns, aged 16 in 1775, would not have agreed. After the (relative) excitements of Kirkoswald, life back home seemed much duller than before, and the farmwork harder than ever. Robert's father now relied on him and Gilbert for the heavy labour. Money was short, as always. The family's future looked harsh and uncertain.

Robert became moody, silent, sullen. He felt trapped and rebellious. He had headaches.

Although he still read all he could, including great – and trashy – novels, he was bored, depressed and miserable. He thought of running away to be a soldier.

He was saved – like so many teenagers before and since – by his friends. And by songs. And by love.

friendship first

In 1777, when Robert was 18, the Burnes family left Mount Oliphant and leased a farm at Lochlie,[1] near the linen-weaving village of Tarbolton. At first the villagers were wary, but Robert soon got to know other young men from workshops and farms. At night, they met to laugh and flirt with girls, lounge at street corners, or roam the countryside.

Robert's new friends were rough and sometimes coarse, just like himself. He knew his manners needed polish. So, late in 1777, he enrolled in country-dancing classes, defying his father's wishes. The dancing was innocent

1. now spelled Lochlea.

enough, and Robert thoroughly enjoyed it, but the rift between him and his stern, moral parent never healed entirely. Later, unfairly, Robert blamed this quarrel for his 'social and amorous madness' in the years that followed.

In his brighter, calmer, more constructive moods, Robert realised that he wanted more from life than dancing and flirting. He must sharpen his wits and stretch his mind. So, in 1780, with Gilbert and five others, he set up a Bachelors' Club, to meet once a week at the local inn. Meetings began with discussion or debate, and ended with a round or two of beer.

A clear head for writing

Today, with disastrous Scottish drinking statistics in mind, biographers sometimes accuse Robert Burns of being a hopeless alcoholic. Robert did enjoy a few mugs of beer or drams of whisky, rum or brandy, and did occasionally 'drown his sorrows' – but, compared with many modern Scots, he was remarkably abstemious. Getting very drunk did not suit him; it only made him sick. His poems and songs – even those praising drink – were mostly composed while sober:

> 'Twill make a man forget his woe;
> 'Twill heighten all his joy:
> 'Twill make the widow's heart to sing,
> Tho' the tear were in her eye...

> *'John Barleycorn', 1782*

The notion that Burns was a drunkard is not a new one. It was encouraged by one of his first biographers, James Currie – a doctor and reformed alcholic, who published an account of Burns's career in 1802. Currie tended to blame all the problems of Burns's life, from his early love-affairs to his last, fatal, illness, on the 'demon drink'.

Burning issues

Membership of the Bachelors' Club was open to 'professed lover[s] of the female sex', and debates there naturally touched on topics dear to local lads' hearts. And, though poor and powerless,[2] the Bachelors weren't stupid. Debating topics ranged from politics, education and philosophy – 'Do we derive more happiness from love or friendship?' – to the unromantic realities of farming life. Robert proposed the first 'problem' for discussion:

'Suppose a young man, bred a farmer, but without any fortune, has it in his power to marry either of two women, the one a girl of large fortune, but neither handsome in person not agreeable in conversation, but who can manage the household affairs of a farm well enough: the other of them a girl every way agreeable in person, conversation, and behaviour, but without any fortune – which of them shall he choose?'

2. *Working-class people did not have the vote.*

The Brotherhood

In 1781, Robert decided to seek new, more mature friends and social contacts – men who just might, one day, help him escape from 'the cheerless gloom' he often felt on the farm. So he joined the Tarbolton Freemasons' Lodge. He was attracted by the brotherhood's promise of fellowship, support and equality. To many villagers, Freemasonry was a dangerously liberal organisation, but Burns remained a loyal Mason for the rest of his life, at times playing a leading part in local Masonic business.

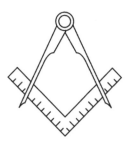

Artwork: MesserWoland/Wikimedia Commons

Braveheart

In spite of making new friends, Robert still enjoyed long country walks alone. One Sunday afternoon, after reading a famous old epic, the *Life of William Wallace* by Blind Harry (lived c.1440–1492), he tramped to woods near Tarbolton where the ancient Scottish hero had hidden from his pursuers. He felt deeply moved to think of the brave, doomed warrior sheltering there, crouched and wary, maybe on the very ground where he himself was now standing.

Years later, remembering that afternoon and in honour of 'Braveheart' William Wallace (d.1305), Robert Burns composed Scotland's favourite patriotic poem:

> Scots, wha hae wi' Wallace bled,
> Scots, wham Bruce has aften led,
> Welcome to your gorie bed
>   Or to victorie!
>
> Now's the day, and now's the hour;
> See the front o' battle lour,
> See approach proud Edward's power –
>   Chains and slaverie!

wha hae: who have.   wham: whom.   aften: often.

lour: loom menacingly.   proud Edward: Edward I of England (reigned 1272–1307), 'Hammer of the Scots'.   power: army.

Wha will be a traitor knave?
Wha can fill a coward's grave?
Wha sae base as be a slave? –
    Let him turn and flee!

Wha for Scotland's King and Law,
Freedom's sword will strongly draw,
Freeman stand or freeman fa' –
    Let him follow me!

By Oppression's woes and pains,
By your sons in servile chains,
We will drain our dearest veins
    But they shall be free!

Lay the proud usurpers low!
Tyrants fall in every foe!
Liberty's in every blow!
    Let us do, or die!

'Scots, Wha Hae', 1793

fa': fall.

Words of love

Whatever else he was doing, young Robert was almost always thinking about poetry. As we saw on page 50, he began writing very early – the first poem we know of dates from 1773, when Robert was only 14. He created it for 'a bonnie, sweet, sonsie[3] lass', Nelly Kirkpatrick, who he worked with that harvest-time.

Like Robert's mother, Nelly sang as she worked. She told him how local girls envied one of their friends, whose admirer – a rich farmer's son – had written verses to praise her. Robert was intrigued. Was this the way to a young woman's heart? In any case, Burns liked a challenge: 'I saw no reason why I might not rhyme as well as he.'

Robert asked Nelly to sing her favourite tune, and wrote these words to go with it:

3. *pleasant, agreeable.*

59

Once I lov'd a bonnie lass,
   Ay, and I love her still;
And whilst that virtue warms my breast,
   I'll love my handsome Nell.

As bonnie lasses I hae seen,
   And mony full as braw;
But, for a modest gracefu' mein,
   The like I never saw.

...

A gaudy dress and gentle air
   May slightly touch the heart;
But it's innocence and modesty
   That polishes the dart.

'Tis this in Nelly pleases me,
   'Tis this enchants my soul;
For absolutely in my breast
   She reigns without control.

'Once I Lov'd a Bonnie Lass', 1773

mony: many.   braw: handsome.

gentle: well-bred.
*dart: Cupid's arrow, which causes people to fall in love – another
classical allusion.*

Not a great poem, but Nelly was delighted.
Who wouldn't be?

Out of this world

Poetry is an art that can be practised anywhere. It needs nothing – except genius. Later in life, Robert recalled how he worked at his verses as he tramped through the mud behind the plough, or puzzled over other poems he had read as he struggled with heavy, routine jobs around the farm. While the monotonous labour tired his body, it freed his mind to think and his heart to feel. Reading and writing poetry lifted his spirits – and gave him glimpses of other possible worlds.

'Thus with me began love and poetry, which at times have been my only, and till within the last twelve months have been my highest, enjoyment...'

Robert Burns, looking back in 1787

O, clappin's good in Febarwar
   An kissin's sweet in May:
But what signifies a young man's love,
   An't dinna last for ay?

O, kissin' is the key o' love
   An clappin' is the lock;
An makin' o's the best thing
   That e'er a young thing got!

from 'O, Can Ye Labour Lea',
a traditional song collected
and adapted by Burns, 1792

clappin': stroking.   an't: if it.   dinna: doesn't.
for ay: for ever.   e'er: ever.   labour lea: plough virgin
land /labour for a long time.

As with many of the lyrics that Burns
collected, there is a more explicit
version of this song.

CHAPTER FOUR

'THAT DELICIOUS PASSION'

By his own admission, teenage Robert Burns was not immediately preposessing. Indeed, he described himself, around 1777, as 'perhaps the most ungainly, awkward boy in the parish – no hermit was less acquainted with the ways of the world'. But as events soon proved, he was a very quick learner. His nights out with the Tarbolton lads and his ready acceptance by the Freemasons showed him that he had a gift for making male friends easily. And it seemed that there was also something about him that appealed – very much – to the lasses.

A heart on fire

'I was generally a welcome guest where I visited ...[and]...where two or three met together, there was I among them. But far beyond all other impulses of my heart was a leaning toward the adorable half of humankind. My heart was completely tinder, and was eternally lighted up by some goddess or other; and, as in every other warfare in this world, my fortune was various; sometimes I was received with favour, and sometimes I was mortified with a repulse...'

Robert Burns, remembering his youth in 1787

'Uncommon invitin''

Way back in 1774, 'Handsome Nell' had let Robert hold her hand and soothe her nettle-stings in the cornfield. Soon after, in 1775, while Robert was at school in Kirkoswald, a 13-year-old servant named Peggy Thomson – whom he first glimpsed through his classroom window – had agreed to join him for delightful walks in the moonlight:

But, Peggy dear, the evening's clear,
    Thick flies the skimming swallow;
The sky is blue, the fields in view,
    All fading green and yellow;
Come, let us stray our gladsome way,
    And view the charms of nature;
The rustling corn, the fruited thorn,
    And every happy creature.

from 'Now Westlin' Winds', 1775[1]

So, just what was this power to attract even the youngest women? Did it spring from Robert's eagerness for friendship, his earnest conversation, his fund of stories old and new, his independent opinions, or his ribald, wicked wit? Was it provoked by his rebellious streak, or his love of animals, or his surprising tenderness towards his younger brothers and sisters?

And what about his looks? Observers agreed that, while Burns was not handsome, he was certainly attractive...

---

1. The fact that the poem is in English rather than Scots perhaps reflects the fact that Burns was attending an English-speaking school at the time.

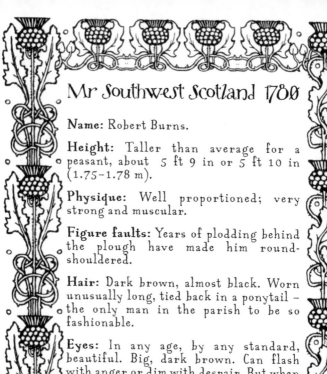

Mr Southwest Scotland 1780

Name: Robert Burns.

Height: Taller than average for a peasant, about 5 ft 9 in or 5 ft 10 in (1.75–1.78 m).

Physique: Well proportioned; very strong and muscular.

Figure faults: Years of plodding behind the plough have made him round-shouldered.

Hair: Dark brown, almost black. Worn unusually long, tied back in a ponytail – the only man in the parish to be so fashionable.

Eyes: In any age, by any standard, beautiful. Big, dark brown. Can flash with anger or dim with despair. But when they glow with passion, few seem able to resist them. Heavy dark brows.

Face: Lower face rounded, with a dimple or cleft in the chin; hint of double chin; mouth and nose large and bold; high forehead; swarthy, weatherbeaten complexion.

Burns in 1787, after a painting by Alexander Nasmyth. Courtesy of the University of Texas Libraries, The University of Texas at Austin.

Whiskers: Clean-shaven but locks of hair curl on either side of his face, together with bushy side-whiskers.

Hands and feet: Big.

Voice: Deep, musical, very expressive.

Robert was, for a poor farmer's son, unusually interested in clothes (although in everything else he was eternally, exasperatingly untidy). And – this is very important – he cared not only for clothes of his own. He noticed, and admired, what women wore. His female friends were gratified and flattered. For himself, he fastened his russet-coloured plaid[2] around his shoulders in a fancy new way, and, when he could afford it, chose his own garments with care:

My coat and my vest, they are Scotch of the best;
O' pairs o' guid breeks I have twa, man,
And stockings and pumps to put on my stumps,
And ne'er a wrong steek in them a', man.

My sarks they are few, but five of them new –
Twal hundred, as white as the snaw, man!
A ten-shillings hat, a Holland cravat –
There are no monie Poets sae braw, man!

from 'The Ronalds of the Bennals', 1780

guid: good.   breeks: breeches.   twa: two.   pumps: flat-heeled shoes.
steek: stitch.   sarks: shirts.   twal hundred: finely woven, with 1,200
threads per width of cloth.   snaw: snow.   Holland: stiff white cloth.
no monie: not many.   braw: fine.

2. a length of woollen cloth, sometimes tartan or chequered, worn as a
shawl or cloak or used as a blanket. Burns's choice of russet red was
unusual – and showy. A definite fashion statement!

Visitors! Home~comers! Long~lost relatives!

As you travel across Bonnie Scotland, admiring its wild scenery, ancient castles, fine cities, quaint whisky distilleries, swinging kilts and mysterious sporrans, try this little game whenever you reach a heritage centre, ceildh bar or any other tartan-trimmed tourist attraction.

How many images of Burns can you spot – and attached to which unlikely objects? We're offering no prizes, but we think we once saw Burns's giant face projected onto a huge old building, though we fear we may have been hallucinating.[3]

NB: Tea-towels and shortbread tins get no points – they are too easy!

---

3. *We were not – it really happened, at Glasgow City Chambers in January 2009.*

'As willin' as I...'

There was another reason, too, why the lasses liked Robert. Today we might call it something passion-killing, such as 'emotional intelligence'. Or perhaps, more glamorously, 'soul'. Here was a man in touch with his feelings – and his libido.

Poetry is not the same as real life, but Burns's words do sometimes reflect his own experience or shed light on his attitudes. Shockingly so, to modern readers, though it is obviously unfair to judge the past by today's standards. More than once, Burns seems to suggest that prowess in bed (or under a haystack, or in a briar bush) is fair recompense for all other misbehaviour. After a literal or metaphorical 'roll in the hay', he expects to be adored, obeyed, or, at the very least, forgiven.

However, following folksong tradition, Burns's poems also cheerfully admit (indeed, they relish the fact) that women can and may demand satisfaction. He admires women's tender care. He praises their skills. He celebrates their charms. He will do his manly best to please them. He does not blame women for seeking love – but they must expect to take the consequences:

> Waes me that e'er I made your bed!
>   Waes me that e'er I saw ye!
> For nou I've lost my maidenheid,
>   An I ken na how they ca' ye.
>
> My name's weel kend in my ain countrie,
>   They ca' me the linkin laddie;
> An ye haed na been as willin as I,
>   Shame fa' them wad e'er hae bade ye.

from 'The Linkin Laddie', after 1787

*Waes me: woe is me.   nou: now.   ken na: don't know.
how they ca' ye: what your name is.   kend: known.   ain: own.
linkin: dancing (euphemism).   An ye haed na: if you had not been.
Shame fa' them wad e'er hae bade ye: Shame on them who ever asked you.*

In an age of primitive contraception and moral double standards, these attitudes made Robert, from the female point of view, more than a little 'dangerous to know'. He fathered 14 children – that we know of – by five different women (see pages 134–135). One, perhaps two, of his girlfriends died in childbirth. And he was never, ever, faithful.

An understanding partner

A modern writer has remarked that Burns's wife's later, easy, acceptance of his countless love-affairs 'seems occasionally to border on the cataleptic'.[4]

It seems that Mrs Burns saw it differently:

'Our Robin should have hud twa wives.'

Jean Armour (Mrs Robert Burns), on agreeing to take in Ann Park's baby daughter (see page 135)

4. A. L. Kennedy, quoted in Robert Crawford, The Bard: Robert Burns, A Biography.

Our dearest blessing

From Robert's own perspective, however, love was 'the first of human joys, our dearest blessing here below!' It was also inseparable from his poetry. Love inspired his writings; his poems and songs encouraged love. And, whether the girls in his arms cared or not, few poets have ever been able to express the deepest feelings of the heart so simply and so truly:

O my luve's like a red, red rose,
  That's newly sprung in June.
O, my luve's like a melodie,
  That's sweetly play'd in tune.

So fair art thou, my bonie lass,
  So deep in luve am I,
And I will luve thee still, my Dear,
  Till a' the seas gang dry.

Till a' the seas gang dry, my Dear
  And the rocks melt wi' the sun!
O I will luve thee still, my Dear,
  While the sands of life shall run.

And fare thee weel, my only Luve,
  And fare thee weel a while!
And I will come again my Luve,
  Tho' it were ten thousand mile!

'A Red, Red Rose', 1794.

gang: go.

'Love is all around you...'

The Ayrshire countryside may have been bleak at times, but it offered lovers like Robert ample space for seduction, either close to home...

> There grows a bonnie brier bush
>   in our kail-yard,
> There grows a bonnie brier bush
>   in our kail-yard;
> And below the bonnie brier bush
>   there's a lassie and a lad,
> And they're busy busy courting
>   in our kail-yard...

> *'The Bonnie Briar Bush', traditional,*
> *collected by Burns c.1793*

kail-yard: vegetable garden (kail is a type of cabbage).
brier: either wild rose or bramble (blackberry).

... or further afield:

It was upon a Lammas night,
When corn rigs are bonnie,
Beneath the moon's unclouded light,
I held awa' to Annie;
The time flew by, wi' tentless heed;
Till, 'tween the late and early,
Wi' sma' persuasion she agreed
To see me thro' the barley.

(Chorus:)

Corn rigs, an' barley rigs,
An corn rigs are bonnie:
I'll ne'er forget that happy night,
Amang the rigs wi' Annie.

The sky was blue, the wind was still,
The moon was shining clearly;
I set her down, wi' right good will,
Amang the rigs o' barley:
I ken't her heart was a' my ain
I lov'd her most sincerely;
I kiss'd her owre and owre again,
Amang the rigs o' barley...

'Corn Rigs Are Bonnie', c.1779

Lammas: a harvest festival in early August.   corn: oats.
rigs: strips of cultivated farmland.   held awa' to: went to see.
tentless: careless.   sma': very little.   amang: among.   ken't: knew.
ain: own.   owre: over.

The personal
and the political

Sometimes love was light-hearted, as in so many of Burns's songs. Sometimes it was heartfelt and deeply serious. But for Burns, and perhaps for many other poor, powerless men and women like him, love was also where they found freedom. In love, rich and poor, male and female, had an equal chance: to sigh, to smile, to yield, to yearn – and to find pleasure.

Tho' women's minds like winter winds
    May shift and turn, an' a' that,
The noblest breast adores them maist –
    A consequence, I draw that.

Great love I bear to a' the fair,
    Their humble slave, an' a' that;
But lordly will, I hold it still
    A mortal sin to thraw that.

...

Their tricks an' craft hae put me daft,
    They've taen me in an' a' that,
But clear your decks, and here's: 'The Sex!'
    I like the jads for a' that !

'Tho' Women's Minds', 1790

maist: most.   thraw: contradict.   jads: jades (girls).
taen: taken.

A model poet?

An exchange from *The Scotsman* newspaper,
5 January 2009:

- 'Burns was a drunk, misogynistic, racist
  philanderer...we have to wonder whether this
  is the right image for modern Scotland.'

  Historian and journalist Michael Fry

- 'This is complete rubbish...Burns' poetry
  spoke about the wealth of human
  experience...he's not a role model, he's a
  great poet.'

  Poet and playwright Liz Lochhead

- 'What signifies the life o' man,
  An 'twere not for the lasses, O...'

  Robert Burns, 'Green Grow the Rashes, O',
  1783

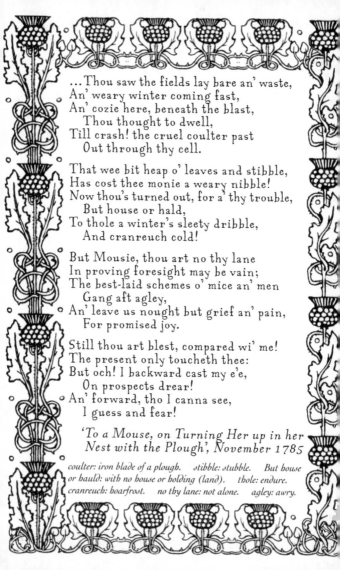

...Thou saw the fields lay bare an' waste,
An' weary winter coming fast,
An' cozie here, beneath the blast,
    Thou thought to dwell,
Till crash! the cruel coulter past
    Out through thy cell.

That wee bit heap o' leaves and stibble,
Has cost thee monie a weary nibble!
Now thou's turned out, for a' thy trouble,
    But house or hald,
To thole a winter's sleety dribble,
    And cranreuch cold!

But Mousie, thou art no thy lane
In proving foresight may be vain;
The best-laid schemes o' mice an' men
    Gang aft agley,
An' leave us nought but grief an' pain,
    For promised joy.

Still thou art blest, compared wi' me!
The present only toucheth thee:
But och! I backward cast my e'e,
    On prospects drear!
An' forward, tho I canna see,
    I guess and fear!

'To a Mouse, on Turning Her up in her
Nest with the Plough', November 1785

coulter: iron blade of a plough.   stibble: stubble.   But house
or hauld: with no house or holding (land).   thole: endure.
cranreuch: hoarfrost.   no thy lane: not alone.   agley: awry.

CHAPTER FIVE

'I GUESS AND FEAR'

When, in 1785, the poor 'wee, sleekit, cowrin, tim'rous beastie' (opposite) was left homeless by a chance swerve of the poet's plough, Burns himself, just like the Mousie, was facing a future full of perplexity. Only one part of his life was going well – his writing. There, he felt increasingly confident of his powers. For the rest, there were only 'guesses and fears'.

In 1781, Burns had left Lochlie and gone to the nearby town of Irvine, to learn the trade of flax-dressing. Flax was one of the improvers' favourite new crops, but it was hard to make money just by growing it. Dressing (processing) added value. Robert did not like the work and soon became ill – first with fever, then with pleurisy.[1] He had terrible nightmares, and, deeply depressed – one biography suggests he suffered a nervous breakdown – feared that he might die. He recovered after several miserable weeks in bed, but worse was to follow. As the flaxmaster and his friends celebrated New Year 1782, 'Our workshop burnt to ashes and left me, like a true poet, not worth sixpence.'[2]

1. *possibly caused by the recommended fever cure: plunging into a cold tub of water, then climbing back into bed, soaking wet and shivering.*
2. *Burns, writing in 1787.*

Life-savers

Determined not to give in, Burns found new lodgings and a new master. He also met two friendly, generous souls who saved, if not his life, then at least his sanity. The first was Mr Templeton, owner of the Irvine bookshop, who let Burns sit among the shelves and read to his heart's content. In particular, Burns was delighted to encounter the *Scottish Poems* of Robert Fergusson (1750–1774), a tragic young writer who had died in the Edinburgh Bedlam[3] aged only 24. Like Burns, Fergusson wrote in Scots, about things he himself had seen or felt, instead of imitating artificial, academic, English poetic fashions.

The second 'saviour' was a sailor, Richard Brown. He had fantastic tales to tell of his travels overseas and his adventures with the lasses. He was a bad influence but good company. He was also most impressed when Robert recited some examples of his poems. Brown was the first to suggest that Burns should publish his work for the whole world to enjoy.

3. *mental asylum; more like a prison than a hospital.*

The call of duty

So, at last, life at Irvine felt better. But Robert could not stay there for ever. His father was now gravely ill with TB; help was needed on the farm. In 1782 Robert went home to do his duty. He was determined, however, not to forget his dreams of a better life, somewhere, someday. In 1783 he began to keep a commonplace book; possibly, he had plans to publish it. It contained 'Observations, Hints, Songs, scraps of Poetry etc by Robert Burnes, a man who has little art in making money, and still less in keeping it'.

Robert was not the only member of his family with money worries. His father had spent the past two years in a dispute with his landlord. Legal fees had used up almost all his money; would he soon be bankrupt?[4] Friendly local lawyer Gavin Hamilton stepped in at the last minute. He let Robert and Gilbert rent one of his own small farms, at Mossgiel near Mauchline, separately from their father. Thanks to this arrangement, after the old

4. Yes, the following year.

man's death the Burnes brothers – and the whole Burnes family – would still have a roof over their heads.

William Burnes passed away early in 1784. Until then, Robert, Gilbert and the younger children all worked hard to keep Lochlie going. So did Agnes Broun – and her maid, Lizzie Paton. Lizzie was young and strong, pleasant and friendly – and the inevitable happened. Not long after William died, she presented Robert with a daughter. Robert was defiantly delighted:

> Thou's welcome, wean! Mishanter fa' me,
> If thoughts o' thee or yet thy mammie,
> Sall ever daunton me or awe me,
>   My sweet, wee lady,
> Or if I blush when thou shalt ca' me,
>   Tyta or daddie!
>
> What tho' they ca' me fornicator,
> An tease thy name in kintra clatter?
> The mair they talk, I'm kend the better;
>   E'n let them clash!
> An auld wife's tongue's a feckless matter
>   To gie ane fash.

wean: child.   Mishanter: mishap.   fa': befall.
daunton me: hold me back.   Tyta: father (an affectionate nickname).

kintra clatter: country gossip.   clash: chatter.   feckless: pointless.
To gie ane fash: to give anyone bother or worry.

Welcome, my bonie, sweet wee dochter!
Tho' ye come here a wee unsought for,
And tho your coming I hae fought for
  Baith kirk and queir;
Yet, by my faith ye're no unwrought for –
  That I shall swear!

Sweet fruit of monie a merry dint,
My funny toil is no a' tint:
Tho' thou cam to the warl' asklent,
  Which fools may scoff at,
In my last plack thy part's be in't
  The better half o't.

Tho I should be the waur bestead,
Thou's be as braw and bienly clad,
And thy young years as nicely bred
  Wi' education,
As onie brat o' wedlock's bed,
  In a' thy station.

Wee image o' my bonie Betty,
As fatherly I kiss and daut thee,
As dear and near my heart I set thee
  Wi' as guid will,

*kirk and queir: church and choir – he has been punished in church for
immorality.   no unwrought for: not unprovided for.*

*dint: bout.   funny: enjoyable.   no a' tint: not all in vain.
warl': world.   asklent: irregularly.   plack: coin
thy part's be in't: your share in it will be.*

*waur bestead: worse off.   braw and bienly: fine and comfortably/
suitably.*

daut: pet.   guid: good.

As a' the priests had seen me get thee
    That's out o' Hell.

Gude grant that thou may ay inherit
Thy mither's looks an' graceful merit,
An' thy poor, worthless daddie's spirit
    Without his failins!
'Twill please me more to see thee heir it
    Than stocket mailins.

And if thou be what I wad hae thee,
An' tak the counsel I shall gie thee,
I'll never rue my trouble wi' thee –
    The cost nor shame o't –
But be a loving father to thee,
    An brag the name o't.

'Welcome to a Bastart Wean', 1784

get: beget.

Gude: God.   *ay: always.*   *stocket mailins: well-stocked farms.*

wad: would.   *gie: give.*

News flash

ROBERT BURNS' BASTART WEAN AUCTIONED FOR £17,400

On 30 March 2011 *The Scotsman* reported that the autograph manuscript of this poem, folded to make 4 pages, had been sold in London the previous day for £17,400.

In disgrace

As planned, the Burnes family moved to the newly rented farm at Mossgiel – all, that is, except Lizzie. She went home to her widowed mother; Robert would not marry her. She stood for all that he was trying to rise above and get away from.

Agnes Broun agreed to raise the 'bastart', but other people in Mauchline were not so tolerant. In the eyes of the Kirk, Robert and Lizzie were guilty of the sin of fornication. For three consecutive Sundays, they had to stand in church in front of friends and neighbours while the Minister lectured them on their shameful lack of self-control. Sulkily, Robert submitted – but later he got his revenge (see pages 88–89). And, as a deliberate insult to authority, he set up a 'Club of Fornicators'. Only fathers of 'irregular' children could join.

From the Kirk's point of view, worse was to come – but Burns had bigger worries. The farm at Mossgiel was in trouble. His mind was full of poetry; he spent hours wandering about rather than working. He began to confide his

thoughts about hypocritical Kirk 'worthies' –
and his own hopes and fears – in poems and
verse letters to his friends:

> There's ay wee faut they whiles lay to me,
> I like the lasses – God forgive me!
> For monie a plack they wheedle from me
>   At dance or fair:
> Maybe some ither thing they gie me
>   They weel can spare.

from 'Epistle to J. Lapraik', 1785

ay: one.   faut: fault.   whiles lay to me: sometimes accuse me of.
monie: many.   plack: coin.   ither: other.   gie: give.   weel: well.

> Ye high, exalted virtuous dames,
>   Tied up in godly laces,
> Before ye gie poor Frailty names,
>   Suppose a change o' cases:
> A dear lov'd lad, convenience snug,
>   A treach'rous inclination –
> But let me whisper in your lug
>   Ye're aiblins nae temptation.

from 'Address to the Unco' Good', 1786

gie: give.   a change o' cases: different circumstances.   lug: ear.
aiblins: maybe.   nae: no.

In another poem from this period, hypocritical
Kirk leader 'Holy Willie' is praying:

O Thou, who in the heavens does dwell,
Who, as it pleases best Thysel',
Sends ane to heaven an' ten to hell,
   A' for Thy glory,
And no for ony gude or ill
   They've done afore Thee!

I bless and praise Thy matchless might,
When thousands Thou hast left in night,
That I am here afore Thy sight,
   For gifts an' grace
A burning and a shining light
   To a' this place.
...

Yet here I am, a chosen sample,
To show Thy grace is great and ample;
I'm here a pillar o' Thy temple,
   Strong as a rock,
A guide, a buckler, and example,
   To a' Thy flock!

But yet, O Lord, confess I must:
At times I'm fash'd wi' fleshly lust:
An' sometimes, too, in warldly trust,
   Vile self gets in:
But Thou remembers we are dust,
   Defiled with sin.

ane: one.   *A': all.*

buckler: shield.

fash'd: troubled.   *wi': with.*   *warldly: worldly.*

O Lord! yestreen, Thou kens, wi' Meg –
Thy pardon I sincerely beg –
O, may't ne'er be a living plague
   To my dishonour!
An' I'll ne'er lift a lawless leg
   Again upon her.

Besides, I farther maun avow –
Wi' Leezie's lass, three times, I trow –
But, Lord, that Friday I was fou,
   When I cam near her,
Or else, Thou kens, Thy servant true
   Wad never steer her.

...

But, Lord, remember me an' mine
Wi' mercies temp'ral an' divine,
That I for grace an' gear may shine,
   Excell'd by nane,
And a' the glory shall be thine,
   Amen, Amen!

from 'Holy Willie's Prayer', 1785

yestreen: yesterday evening.   kens: knows.
may't ne'er: may it never.

maun: must.   trow: declare.   fou: drunk.   wad: would.
steer: meddle with.

temp'ral: temporal (worldly).   gear: goods.

'O Jeany...'

It was around this time, early in 1785, that Burns met the woman he loved – in his own way, when it suited him – for the rest of his life. Her name was Jean Armour. She was the daughter of a stonemason in Mauchline, and was later described by visitors to Burns's house as 'very comely...with plain sound sense and very good manners'.

Burns being the man he was, and human nature ditto, it was not too long before Jean discovered that she was pregnant.[5] This was a real scandal; Jean was not some servant-girl who could be sent home and forgotten. Her father was a leading member of the Mauchline community; a skilled, successful tradesman, and a Freemason. When he heard of his daughter's condition, he fainted clean away.

5. Burns's feelings at this time are not clear; at first he described Jean, mockingly, as a 'hen' he had 'brought down with his gun' (oh dear!). But just a few months later, he wrote (see page 94) that he was passionately in love with her.

90

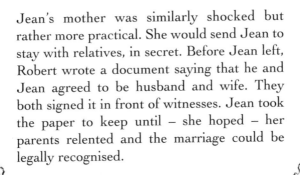

Love me, love my dog...

Jean first set eyes on Robert Burns as he strolled across Mauchline green – the girls spread their washing on the grass to dry, so what better place for a young man to wander? His favourite, muddy, collie dog ran across the clean clothes, and so Jean chased it away. Burns replied, 'Lassie, if you thought ought o'me, ye wadna hurt my dog!'

Soon after, Jean remembered, she saw Burns at a dance 'and we fell acquainted'. Aged just 19, Jean had a pleasing face, a nice voice (she was another good singer), shapely legs[6] and a fashionable hourglass figure. Burns arranged to meet her after nightfall.

6. The girls hitched up their long skirts while they worked.

Jean's mother was similarly shocked but rather more practical. She would send Jean to stay with relatives, in secret. Before Jean left, Robert wrote a document saying that he and Jean agreed to be husband and wife. They both signed it in front of witnesses. Jean took the paper to keep until – she hoped – her parents relented and the marriage could be legally recognised.

Robert also wrote a song for Jean (with himself as the hero; who else?):

> Oh wha my babie-clouts will buy?
> Wha will tent me when I cry?
> Wha will kiss me where I lie?
> The rantin dog, the daddie o't.
>
> Wha will own he did the faut?
> What will buy my groaning maut?
> Wha will tell me how to ca't?
> The rantin dog, the daddie o't.
>
> When I mount the creepie-chair,
> Wha will sit beside me there?
> Gie me Rob, I'll seek nae mair,
> The rantin dog, the daddie o't.
>
> Wha will crack me to my lane?
> Wha will mak me fidgin fain?
> Wha will kiss me o'er again?
> The rantin dog, the daddie o't.

'The Rantin Dog, the Daddie o't', c.1785

clouts: clothes.   tent: tend, care for.   rantin': wild.   o't: of it.

faut: fault   groaning maut: malt to brew beer for the midwife.
ca't: call (name) it.

creepie-chair: low chair or stool (to sit on to give birth).
nae mair: no more.

crack me to my lane: walk and talk with me alone.
fidgin fain: wild with desire.

Jean's parents were furious. They would not accept a failing tenant farmer with no prospects and a dubious poetic reputation as their son-in-law. Bullied and browbeaten, Jean handed over the precious document – and the Armours' family lawyer destroyed it. Jean's parents told Robert that she no longer wanted to see him.

Robert could not bear it. Jean had betrayed him. She had rejected his love. Damn the Armours! Damn their lawyer! Damn Jean!

further afield

Even before Robert met Jean, he knew he could not stay much longer in Mauchline. What with love and poetry, he was not pulling his weight on the farm. He planned to give his share to brother Gilbert, a calmer, steadier worker, and – like so many Scots at that time – leave his homeland to seek his fortune on the other side of the world. Burns went to see a man whose brother ran a plantation[6] in Jamaica. Could he, too, find a job overseas?

6. *Yes, worked by African slaves – see page 161.*

'A grand cure'

Never man loved, or rather, adored, woman more than I did her [Jean]...how happy I have been in her arms!....May God forgive her ingratitude....

I have run into all kinds of dissipation and riot...to drive her out of my head....And now for a grand cure; the ship is on her way home that is to take me out to Jamaica; and then farewell dear old Scotland! and farewell dear ungrateful Jean!

Robert Burns, writing to a friend in 1786

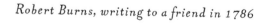

Highland Mary

Robert knew that it might take months to hear from Jamaica. Meanwhile, his heart was aching. Where better to seek consolation than in another woman's embraces? In April 1786 he found himself thinking of a stranger he had met – in church – just a few months ago. She was a dairymaid from Cowal, north of Glasgow: a land of lochs and mountains. Her name was Mary Campbell, 'Highland Mary'.

Readers – how did he persuade her? Why did she agree? Mary must have known of Robert's reputation, and yet within a few weeks of their first midnight stroll together, she was (probably) pregnant. One biographer claims that Mary was already another man's mistress; her affair with Robert was just a brief fling. Another supposes that Robert and Mary conducted a traditional Highland 'handfasting' (temporary marriage) ceremony; certainly, they wrote their names in each other's Bibles, which might suggest some sort of commitment. We just don't know.

Burns also proposed, in verse, that he and
Mary run away together to Jamaica, as man
and wife. (Who can say how seriously? Burns
often used poems to play with emotions,
writing words to fit an imaginary or
temporary state of mind):

> Will ye go to the Indies, my Mary,
>   And leave auld Scotia's shore?
> Will ye go to the Indies, my Mary
>   Across th' Atlantic roar?
> …
>
> I hae sworn by the Heavens to my Mary,
>   I have sworn by the Heavens to be true,
> And sae may the Heavens forget me,
>   When I forget my vow!

But that was for the future. Right now,
Highland Mary did the only thing she could:
she went home to her family. While visiting
her brother at Greenock, and nursing his
putrid fever (typhus), Mary herself was
infected, and gave birth prematurely. Mother
and baby both died.

To the unromantic or uncaring, Robert's life
in 1786 might now be likened to a
frantic French farce. For, almost as soon as
Highland Mary left Mauchline, Jean Armour

returned – summoned by the Kirk so that she and Robert could be admonished again for her pregnancy.

Jean did not know what her parents had said to Robert, or how hurt and angry he had been. Nor did she know about Highland Mary. Instead, she wanted Robert to honour the marriage agreement they had made. Robert refused. Here now was something else, as well as money and farming, to make him 'guess and fear'. Was he married to either of these pregnant girls, or even to both of them?[7]

Burns wanted out. His only hope seemed to lie far away, in Jamaica. He had now received the offer of a book-keeping job on a plantation near Port Antonio. But Jean's parents still sought justice. They applied for a warrant to arrest Burns. He would be gaoled unless he could pay to support Jean and her unborn child. That was impossible: Burns was almost penniless. The bold, braw, lover-poet slunk away from Mauchline and hurried into hiding.

7. just possibly, to Jean.

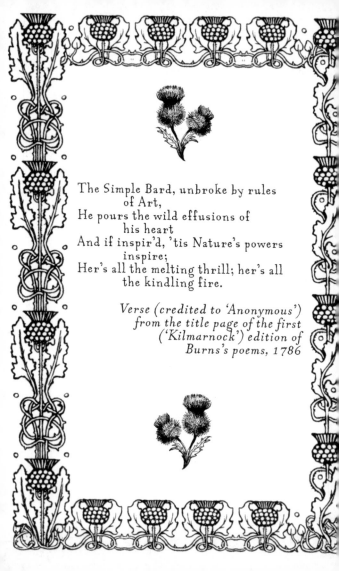

The Simple Bard, unbroke by rules
      of Art,
He pours the wild effusions of
      his heart
And if inspir'd, 'tis Nature's powers
      inspire;
Her's all the melting thrill; her's all
      the kindling fire.

Verse (credited to 'Anonymous')
from the title page of the first
('Kilmarnock') edition of
Burns's poems, 1786

'ONE LAST FOOLISH THING'

two pregnant mistresses (or wives), a failing farm, an aged mother and baby daughter to provide for, plans to emigrate, and the threat of prison would probably have been more than enough to occupy the mind of any ordinary young man.[1] But, as we have seen, Robert Burns was far from that. At the same time as Jean's parents were fulminating and Highland Mary was waiting, Burns was busy taking the most important step so far in his career as a poet. He was preparing to publish!

1. In 1786 Burns was 27.

Before leaving Scotland, maybe for ever, Burns was determined to leave behind 'one last foolish thing' – a book – to be remembered by. So far, his poems had mostly been read or recited to entertain his family, his fellow Freemasons, or the Bachelors, Fornicators and other friends who gathered at local inns. But increasingly, Robert found, he was being asked for copies of favourite works – and these copies were being loaned, sent or otherwise circulated to a wide circle of admiring readers.

Burns was at the peak of his powers. Many of his most famous – and best – poems were composed in the four years between 1784 and 1788. Here are just a few of them:

1784
A Poet's Welcome to his Love-Begotten Daughter
  (also known as 'Welcome to a Bastart Wean')
The Bells of Mauchline

1785
Holy Willie's Prayer
Epistle to J. Lapraik, an Old Scottish Bard
Second Epistle to J. Lapraik
Song: Rantin', Rovin' Robin

The Holy Fair
To a Mouse, on Turning Her up in her Nest
　with the Plough
The Jolly Beggars: A Cantata
The Cottar's Saturday Night
Address to the Deil
Scotch Drink

1786
The Auld Farmer's New-Year-Morning
　Salutation to his Auld Mare, Maggie
The Twa Dogs
Address to the Unco Guid, or the Rigidly
　Righteous
To a Louse, on Seeing One on a Lady's Bonnet,
　at Church
Song: My Highland Lassie, O
Address to a Haggis

1787
Song: Bonnie Dundee
Song: A Bottle and Friend

1788
Up in the Morning Early
Verses to Clarinda
Of A' the Airts the Wind Can Blaw
Song: I Hae a Wife o' my Ain
Auld Lang Syne

Burns enjoyed his local fame; he grew more confident, even arrogant. Gavin Hamilton, his landlord, began to show off his pet poet to literary-minded acquaintances. It was even rumoured that a very respectably lady, having heard her servant sing one of Burns's (thankfully more decorous) love songs, invited the rough ploughman into her drawing room, to congratulate him.

The business of publishing

Yes, a book of poems would make a good and lasting memorial. But how was it to be printed, bound and sold? As carefully crafted objects, with hand-set type, hand-folded, hand-trimmed, hand-made rag paper, and (often) hand-made individual leather bindings, all books were expensive.

Books of poems, in particular, were a luxury, only for the wealthy. Burns could not afford to purchase one – so how could he pay to publish? The only way was by advertising for subscribers: rich patrons who would each advance money to buy a copy before the book was produced.

PROPOSALS
for publishing, by subscription
SCOTTISH POEMS,
by Robert Burns.

The work to be elegantly printed,
in one volume octavo.[2]
Price stitched,[3] three shillings.

As the author has not the most distant
mercenary view in publishing, as soon as so
many subscribers appear as will defray the
necessary expense the work will be sent
to the press.

This modest advertisement was sent out in April 1786; by midsummer, around 350 subscribers had come forward – enough to pay the printer, John Wilson of Kilmarnock. Burns was in business!

2. *a small format, made by folding a sheet of paper to make 8 leaves; the actual size of the book depends on the size of the sheet.*
3. *The signatures (sections) of each volume would be firmly held together by stitching, ready for the purchaser's individual choice of binding, in leather or cloth.*

During the next few weeks, Burns spent a lot of time with the printers, carefully choosing which poems to include or omit,[4] and checking each stage of the production. He went to visit – and charm – more wealthy subscribers. He wrote, and later rather regretted, a preface for the book, in which he portrayed himself as being 'in fear and trembling' now that he had 'presented himself to the public in the character of an Author'. He also protested (perhaps rather too much) that 'just because he can make a shift to jingle a few Scots doggerel rhymes together' that did not mean that he considered himself 'as a Poet of no small consequence'.

In 'presenting' his works to the established literary world, Burns was being modest, as custom demanded. However, his apology for 'Scots doggerel' was expressed in the most correct, elegant, formal English. It rather irritated him that most readers still chose to think of him as an untutored 'peasant poet', rather than recognise him as a man of good taste and sophisticated literary talents.

4. For fear of alienating his subscribers, Burns did not include religious satires or bawdy songs.

fame at last

In any case, Burns's modesty – real or mock –
turned out to be quite unnecessary. His book,
Poems, Chiefly in the Scottish Dialect, 240 pages
long and containing 44 compositions,
appeared on 31 July 1786. It was an instant
success – in the pubs and clubs of Mauchline,
in the solid homes of lawyers and (yes) Kirk
ministers, and in the fine houses of local
gentry. Altogether, 612 copies were printed;
they sold out within a month.

Burns was, of course, very pleased, and also
mightily relieved. He now had enough to pay
for his voyage to Jamaica. His first ship was
delayed, so he booked another passage – to the
wrong harbour on the far side of the island.
After arranging his voyage for a third time,
Burns sent his luggage to the port,[5] picked up
copies of his book – he had promised to deliver
them to distant subscribers – and prepared to
leave Scotland for ever.

5. *Greenock, where Highland Mary would soon die.*

105

Burns spent the first night of his journey with a hospitable Kirk Minister, Mr Lawrie, and his young family.[6] They were alarmed to hear that this exciting new poet was planning to sail away. Lawrie had connections in Edinburgh. Let him show Burns's poems to them! If his friends liked the book, surely Burns could earn his living as a writer, at home here in Scotland? Impressed, excited, but rather doubtful, Robert went back to Mossgiel.

More excitement soon followed, for on 3 September 1786 Jean Armour gave birth – to twins!

> The Hero of these artless strains,
>   A lowly bard was he,
> Who sung his rhymes in Coila's plains
>   Wi' mickle mirth and glee;
> Kind Nature's care had given his share,
>   Large, of the flaming current;
> And, all devout, he never sought
>   To stem the sacred torrent.

Coila: Kyle, southeast Ayrshire.   mickle: great.

6. He composed, right in front of their admiring eyes, verses with the refrain 'Irvine bairns are bonie a'.'

He felt the powerful, high behest,
  Thrill, vital, thro' and thro';
And sought a corresponding breast,
  To give obedience due;
Propitious Powers screen'd the young flow'rs
  From mildews of abortion;
And lo! the bard – a great reward –
  Has got a double portion!

from 'Nature's Law: A Poem', 1786

Emergency equipment for the poet in a hurry

Burns composed verses in his head, playing with patterns of rhymes and rhythms as he plodded behind the plough. Or else he jotted them down on any surface he could find – a banknote, a windowpane. Back at home he copied out each poem in his neat, flowing handwriting, correcting and improving as necessary. He kept copies of all his writings in the little attic bedroom he shared with his brother Gilbert.

Everywhere Burns went, he carried a tiny inkwell, goose-feather quills and a knife to sharpen them, so that he could jot down a new and pleasing phrase or rhyme straight away, before it disappeared.

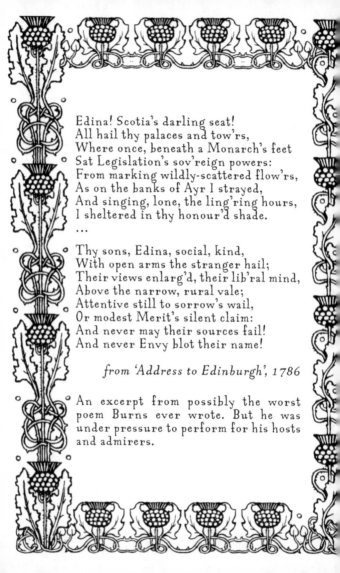

Edina! Scotia's darling seat!
All hail thy palaces and tow'rs,
Where once, beneath a Monarch's feet
Sat Legislation's sov'reign powers:
From marking wildly-scattered flow'rs,
As on the banks of Ayr I strayed,
And singing, lone, the ling'ring hours,
I sheltered in thy honour'd shade.
...

Thy sons, Edina, social, kind,
With open arms the stranger hail;
Their views enlarg'd, their lib'ral mind,
Above the narrow, rural vale;
Attentive still to sorrow's wail,
Or modest Merit's silent claim:
And never may their sources fail!
And never Envy blot their name!

from 'Address to Edinburgh', 1786

An excerpt from possibly the worst
poem Burns ever wrote. But he was
under pressure to perform for his hosts
and admirers.

'CALEDONIA'S BARD'

t he thrill of becoming a father again could not last. And the babies – named Robert and Jean, for their sinful parents – only increased Robert's problems. On the one hand, Jean was still pressing him to marry, and he was still refusing. On the other hand, Highland Mary was still waiting for him, maybe ready to sail to Jamaica. Mr Lawrie had not heard from Edinburgh. And harvest was approaching, when Robert would be needed back on the farm. What, oh what, should he do?

Robert decided to go. Then he decided to stay – at least until Mr Lawrie had finally heard from Edinburgh. At last the reply came. It was from of Scotland's most senior poets, Dr Thomas Blacklock (1721–1791).

Edinburgh's amazing vibrating poet

This is not meant to mock (Dr Blacklock had been blind since childhood) but simply to smile along with a kindly and eccentric friend of Robert Burns.

The good doctor was a teacher, Kirk minister, and helper of poor scholars. He also wrote poetry. He claimed he could only compose his sermons and verses while walking round his room. So that he did not bump into the furniture, he developed a sort of quivering motion, which allowed him to brush gently against objects rather than bang into them. He even wrote about this (badly):

As some vessel tossed by wind and tide
Bounds o'er the waves, and rocks from side
     to side,
In just vibration thus I always move.

An influential admirer

The doctor liked Burns's poems – very much:

'There is a pathos and delicacy in his serious poems, a vein of wit and humour in those of a more festive turn, which cannot be too much admired nor too warmly approved. I think I shall never open the book without feeling my astonishment renewed and increased.'

He also wanted to read more:

'It were much to be wished, for the sake of the young man [Burns], that a second edition, more numerous than the former, could immediately be printed; as it appears certain that its intrinsic merit, and the exertion of the author's friends, might give it a more universal circulation than any thing of the kind which has been published within my memory.'

Now let's hear Burns's own version of what happened next:

'I had taken the last farewell of my few friends...I had composed the last song I should ever measure in Scotland –'The Gloomy night is gathering fast' – when a letter from Dr Blacklock to a friend of mine [Mr Lawrie] overthrew all my schemes, by opening new prospects to my poetic ambition. The Doctor belonged to a set of critics for whose applause I had not dared to hope. His opinion that I would meet with encouragement in Edinburgh for a second edition, fired me so much, that away I posted for that city, without a single acquaintance, or a single letter of introduction.'

Well, yes, and so he did. But first, Burns went to Kilmarnock, to enquire about producing a second edition of his poems there; he found he could not afford it. He had dinner with a (minor, young) lord, eager to make the acquaintance of the local 'genius'. Then, suddenly, tragically, he learned that Highland Mary had died – and that the Campbell family blamed him. 'A wastrel', they said.

Mary's death left Robert completely free to marry Jean Armour. But yet again, he would not. His life had changed; it was still changing. Instead, he borrowed a pony and headed for Edinburgh. He arrived in Scotland's capital on 28 November 1786.

As we saw on page 37, Burns received a warm welcome. Here was a new celebrity! How strong and vigorous! How unspoiled! How natural! Even better, 'untaught' Burns turned out to be polite and dignified, and could converse intelligently on a surprising range of topics. His rough-hewn looks were an adornment to any lady's tea-party; his bawdy wit went down well with the gentlemen at dinners and clubs. He was a breath of fresh air!

A Noble Savage?

Burns's visit to Edinburgh came barely 15 years after French philosopher Jean-Jacques Rousseau (1712–1778) had formulated his concept of the 'Noble Savage', in 1762. Rousseau and his followers believed that 'natural' men and women were better and more noble than those whom civilisation had corrupted. Was Burns living proof of his theories?

Straight to the heart

Burns's poems and songs, too, were unexpected and refreshing. It was not just the language – Robert Fergusson (1750–1774) and Allan Ramsay (1686–1758)[1] had written in Scots before Burns, and Edinburgh readers with a taste for poetry knew (better than Burns did, in fact) the works of great Scots *makars* (national bards), such as William Dunbar (c.1460–c.1520), who had lived in earlier centuries.

No, Burns's appeal lay in his extraordinary ability to touch the hearts of his readers. (As one 21st-century critic put it, Burns's poetry 'makes us feel that we are being talked to by a man right there at our side'.)[2] His verses described, on the surface, real, rough-and-ready everyday life, but underneath they made readers share in the most tender, shocking or tragic of universal human emotions.

---

1. the father of the famous portrait painter of the same name (1713–1784).
2. Novelist and law professor Alexander McCall Smith in the Daily Telegraph, 24 January 2009.

As well, of course, there was Burns's amazing facility with metre, rhyme and rhythm, his verve and daring, his irreverence, ebullience and humour. No-one had written in quite this way before. He was an original.

What they said in Edinburgh

'elegant, simple and pleasing'

The New Annual Register, 1786

'...with what uncommon penetration and sagacity this heaven taught ploughman, from his humble unlettered station, has looked upon men and manners.'

The Lounger, 1786

'...we do not recollect to have ever met with a more signal instance of true and uncultivated genius, than in the author of these Poems....all the rigours of fortune have not been able to repress the frequent efforts of his lively and vigorous imagination...'

The Critical Review, 1787

Watch the bardie

Burns was given the unofficial title 'Caledonia's Bard' by Edinburgh Freemasons. He had already claimed it in his commonplace book, and in his poetry – though, with characteristic wit, he also called himself 'bardie' – a Scots word meaning 'little bard', but also 'prickly, disrespectful, challenging, argumentative'.

Burns probably first met the concept of 'bard' (national poet) in the works of another young Scottish writer, 'Ossian' (James Macpherson, 1736–1796). Macpherson claimed to have discovered and translated ancient Gaelic epic poems, but had in fact composed them himself as a gesture of Scottish pride and to proclaim Scotland's independent identity.

Today, experts do not all agree about Burns's support (or otherwise) for Scotland's independence. But one leading scholar suggests that Burns's deliberate choice of an old Scots metre, the 'habbie',[3] for many of his most important poems 'is crucial to the national spirit of his poetry'.[4]

3. There are examples on pages 78, 83–85, 87 (top), 88–89, 151 (bottom) and 175.
4. Robert Crawford in the Dictionary of National Biography, 2004.

Poet out of place

Burns was flattered by all the attention, but Edinburgh made him uneasy. He felt patronised by the rich and grand, and, at the same time, bored and resentful. His position was paradoxical: he was the one with talent and energy, but he was poor and powerless. His hosts might be (indeed, often were) lazy, dull or foolish, but they had money, influence and leisure to devote to the life of the mind.

On page 108 we can see what happened to at least some of Burns's poetry at this time, when, out of compliment to his hosts, he felt obliged to write in polite English style in praise of their city. As he readily admitted, 'I think my ideas are more barren in English than in Scotch.'

Although 18th-century Edinburgh prided itself on being 'the Athens of the North', it was not, in the 1780s, a particularly exciting place to be. Politically, since 1707, it had been rather a backwater; two of its greatest minds, philosopher David Hume (1711–1776) and economist Adam Smith (1723–1790), had died or were dying.[5] Its top doctor, William Hunter (1718–1783), and top scientist, his brother John (1728–1793), had moved to London; so had its greatest architect, Robert Adam (1728–1792). The next 'new wave' of talent was hardly out of the schoolroom, although Robert Burns did meet the teenage Walter Scott (1771–1832, later a famous novelist), and was impressed by him.

5. *Burns had read both, back home on the farm.*

Scott on Burns

The admiration was mutual. Looking back, here is how Sir Walter Scott remembered Burns:

'His person was strong and robust; his manner rustic, not clownish, a sort of dignified plainness and simplicity which received part of its effect perhaps from knowledge of his extraordinary talents....I think his countenance was more massive than it looks in any of the portraits....there was a strong impression of shrewdness in all his lineaments; the eye alone, I think, indicated the poetical character and temperament....I never saw such another....though I have seen the most distinguished men of my time.'

The Edinburgh edition

Burns went to Edinburgh to further his poetic career. Surely here he would find an enterprising publisher to bear the cost of a second, enlarged edition of his book? He did – the publisher's name was William Creech[6] – and on 17 April 1878 a new, 'Edinburgh' edition of *Poems, Chiefly in the Scottish Dialect* appeared. Within weeks, it earned Burns an astonishing £400; for him, a small fortune.[7]

Very soon afterwards, Burns sold the copyright in the book to Creech for 100 guineas.[8] This was money in his hand, right now (although Creech took a long time to pay it); in return, Creech kept future profits. A good deal? Perhaps, in the short term; but not with the benefit of hindsight.

6. *Burns later called Creech 'a vampire'.*
7. *equivalent to around £42,500 today.*
8. *£105, but worth about £10,500 today.*

A new way to publish old poems

ROBERT BURNS iPHONE APP UPDATED AFTER CRASH PROTESTS

On 30 January 2011 *The Scotsman* reported that the Scottish government's new text-based iPhone app, designed to make Burns's poems available to a new audience worldwide, had been updated after the first version proved unreliable.

According to culture minister Fiona Hyslop, 'This app uses the very latest technology to bring Burns firmly into the 21st century....It is a great platform to promote his work on the international stage.'

It is understood that the new version works well, and there are plans to make it available on other platforms.

While he was in Edinburgh, Burns took the opportunity to travel further, exploring parts of Scotland he had never dreamed of being able to visit. Sometimes he went alone, but usually he was accompanied by one of his new friends from Edinburgh. The purpose of their journeys? Pleasure, of course (they were entertained by many admirers of Burns's work along the way),[9] but also to look at historic places connected with Scotland's brave and glorious past – and to collect more traditional Scottish songs and lyrics.

After touring the Borders in 1787, Burns went back briefly to Mauchline, to see his family, pay off old debts, give Gilbert money to run the farm, and buy (generous) presents for his mother, brothers and sisters. He saw Jean (before his visit was over, she was pregnant again) – and her parents. They had changed their tune and were now embarassingly keen to be connected to such a celebrity. Burns went back to Edinburgh, disgusted.

---

9. *Burns wrote: 'I have fought my way through the savage hospitality of this country, the object of the hosts being to send every guest to bed drunk if they can.'*

Burns's travels

Places visited by Burns between May and September 1787

N

Fochabers
Peterhead
Aberdeen
Inverary
Inverness
Blair Atholl
Loch Lomond
Crieff
Dundee
Edinburgh
Dunbar
Eyemouth
Stirling
Berwick
Glasgow
Melrose
Mauchline
Ayr
Dumfries
Carlisle
Newcastle

122

Mauchline confirmed what Burns had been feeling for some time: he had had enough of farming. He wanted a different job, one that would feed his family and yet leave him time for poetry. So what about the Excise?

As trading ports along the coast of southwest Scotland prospered and flourished, so did smuggling. The Excise service, founded in 1643 to catch and combat smugglers, was expanding. It was a career with a future. Burns must – and did – ask one of his influential Edinburgh friends to find him an Excise position.

At the same time as Burns was thinking about this new and different career, he was also meeting, and flirting with, a new and different class of women. Might his new fame lead to a new kind of love?

Passion and poetry

Her name was Nancy (strictly, Mrs Agnes McLehose) and she was a young, blonde, 'fluffy, full-bosomed'[10] grass widow who adored poetry. She was educated; she had read widely. She had tried writing herself – conventional verses and letters. Her unpleasant husband was working abroad; she had little children. She invited Robert to call at her apartment, one evening, alone, in December 1787. But, alas for Burns's amorous intentions, Nancy also had strict Christian principles.

All that was left for them to share, therefore, were burning gazes, heartfelt sighs, stolen kisses, furtive embraces, passionate letters and poetry. They gave each other poetic names – she Clarinda, he Sylvander – as if they were a nymph and swain in a fashionable pastoral lyric. It was a game, and presumably, they both – at least at first – enjoyed it. Certainly, the intensity of their feelings inspired Burns to create some of the finest poems of love and longing ever written.

And Burns would not have been Burns if, very soon after he had climbed upstairs to sigh elegantly with Clarinda, he had not also gone downstairs to the servants' quarters to make her maid, Jenny Clow, pregnant.

10. *according to Carswell's biography (see page 13).*

Ae fond kiss, and then we sever!
Ae farewell, and then forever!
Deep in heart-wrung tears I'll pledge thee,
Warring sighs and groans I'll wage thee.

Who shall say that Fortune grieves him,
While the star of hope she leaves him?
Me, nae cheerfu' twinkle lights me;
Dark despair around benights me.

I'll nae blame my partial fancy;
Naething could resist my Nancy!
But to see her was to love her,
Love but her, and love forever.

Had we never lov'd sae kindly,
Had we never lov'd sae blindly,
Never met – or never parted –
We had ne'er been broken-hearted.

Fare-thee-weel, thou first and fairest!
Fare-thee-weel, thou best and dearest!
Thine be ilka joy and treasure,
Peace, Enjoyment, Love and Pleasure!

Ae fond kiss, and then we sever!
Ae farewell, alas, forever!
Deep in heart-wrung tears I'll pledge thee,
Warring sighs and groans I'll wage thee.

'Ae Fond Kiss', 1791

Ae: one.   nae: no.   sae: so.   ilka: each.

125

Nature's charms

Ah, pastoral! It's a mood, a game, an elegant pose, a delightful escape from everyday life into a green and pleasant land. There, everything is beautiful; everyone is forever young. There is no sin, no guilt, no disease – but maybe just a few comic peasants to add gritty contrast to the exquisite, heart-breaking, deeply romantic scene.

Burns loved playing the game with Clarinda. He was far from being the first – or the last. Think Ancient Greek and Roman shepherds, piping lonely songs to their flocks. Think Botticelli's painting of Flora, robed in blossoms and stars. Think Shakespeare's *As You Like It* and *A Midsummer Night's Dream*. Think French Queen Marie Antionette, playing with real sheep on her manicured model farm. Think Beethoven's 6th symphony; think Schubert's songs. Think Laura Ashley, c.1973. Think (minus the mud) the Glastonbury Festival...

But back home in his own fields, or on his travels to explore Scotland, Burns's real response to nature was much more honest and true. Many of his finest poems mingle tender love and the Scottish landscape:

Now simmer blinks on flowr'y braes,
And o'er the crystal streamlets plays,
Come, let us spend the lightsome days
In the birks of Aberfeldie!

(Chorus:)

Bonie lassie, will ye go,
Will ye go, will ye go?
Bonie lassie, will ye go
To the birks of Aberfeldie?

The little birdies blithely sing,
While o'er their heads the hazels hing,
Or lightly flit on wanton wing,
In the birks of Aberfeldie!

'The Birks of Aberfeldie', 1787

simmer: summer.   blinks: shines.   braes: slopes.
birks: birch trees.   hing: hang.

And Burns's exuberant letters reveal how
nature thrilled and energised him:

While briers an' woodbines budding green,
And paitricks scraichin loud at e'en
An' morning poussie whiddin seen,
Inspire my Muse...

'Epistle to J. Lapraik', 1785

briers: either wild roses or brambles.   woodbines: honeysuckle.
paitricks scraichin: partridges calling.   e'en: evening.
poussie: hare.   whiddin: scampering, running.·

Searching auld wives' barrels,
  Ochon the day!
That clarty barm should stain my laurels:
  But what'll ye say?
These movin' things ca'd wives an' weans,
Wad move the very hearts o' stanes!

'Extemporaneous Effusion', c.1792

Ochon: alas!   clarty barm: mucky yeast (used in brewing).
stain my laurels: tarnish my reputation as a poet.
ca'd: called.   weans: children.   Wad: would.
stanes: stones.   extemporaneous: made up on the spot.

Burns descibes his work as an Excise
inspector. The job was not smart,
intellectual or even interesting, but it
paid the bills.

'MY LUCKLESS LOT'

Burns may or may not have genuinely loved Clarinda – 'Whatever love means', as another man with a mistress once remarked. But, if Burns was honest with himself, Clarinda could never be part of his future. And now (March 1788) was decision time. He had just been offered a longed-for job with a steady salary by the Excise. Should he take that? Or should he follow the suggestion of Edinburgh banker, traveller, agricultural Improver and amateur inventor, Patrick Miller, to become a tenant on one of his farms?

The decision was even more pressing because Jean's parents, exasperated by her second pregnancy, had banished her from their home. Even if Burns still would not marry Jean, he knew he must provide her and their children with a roof over their heads.

Burns went back to Mauchline, with Clarinda's romantic phrases still buzzing in his brain. In comparison, Jean seemed shabby, ordinary, ignorant, pathetic. He felt depressed – but not too depressed to bed her on a convenient pile of dry horse-litter (and to boast about it afterwards in a letter to one of his male friends). He gave Jean a guinea (£1.05, but worth about £100 today), told her to be 'a good girl', found lodgings for her, and paid for a doctor to attend her in childbirth when the time came. There was not long to wait: Jean had a second set of twins on March 13. They died a few days later.

By now, Burns had almost made up his mind – he would join the Excise, and maybe leave Mauchline for ever. He went to Tarbolton, for six weeks' Excise training. But then (after visiting Mr Miller's farm with an old country friend and advisor) Burns shifted his opinion. He would settle on the land. It was where he belonged! He would take it!

Becoming the tenant of Ellisland farm – for that was the land in question – would also mean leaving Mauchline. Ellisland was further south, close to the market town of Dumfries. And it would mean marriage.

As the old nursery-rhyme says, 'The farmer wants a wife.' If Burns was going to leave elegant Edinburgh for hard work on the land, he must have a woman to share the burden with him. He was not looking for romantic love, but companionship and convenience, mixed perhaps with duty. In April 1788 the marriage of Robert Burns and Jean Armour was formally recognised by the law. It was approved by the Kirk, after payment of a fine, in August the same year. The bride wore black silk – not a sign of mourning, but a status symbol: black was one of the most expensive colours for cloth then available. Burns got it specially for her – 15 yards (13.7 metres)! – all the way from Glasgow.

The new Mrs Burns

'...the handsomest figure, the sweetest temper, the soundest constitution, and kindest heart in the county. Mrs Burns believes, as firmly as her creed, that I am *le plus bel esprit, et le plus honnete homme*[1] in the universe...she has...the finest "wood-note wild"[2] I ever heard.'

Letter from Burns to a woman friend, 1788

1. *the greatest wit and the most refined gentleman.*
2. *singing voice (he is quoting Milton's description of Shakespeare).*

Burns moved to Ellisland in June 1788, leaving Jean at Mauchline. He spent the first months on the farm building a house for his family. Until it was ready, Burns lived in a rough hut – although (presumably not seeing the irony) a neighbouring gentry family, the Riddells, kindly offered him the frivolous, decorative, 'hermitage' summerhouse in their grounds as a place to write his poetry. In return, Burns developed a passionate friendship with Mrs Riddell, 'Maria'.

For the first time in his life (and only briefly), Burns was free of money worries. With the earnings from his Edinburgh edition, he bought furniture, books, livestock, farm tools, seed-corn, a new horse to ride – and more fine clothes for Jean. But before long, he began to curse his 'luckless lot'. Life at Ellisland was a sad come-down from his glory days in Edinburgh. The old rigs were exhausted; the land was sour, the whole farm needed expensive new dykes (stone walls) and drains. The first harvest was disastrous, so Burns decided to change from arable farming to raising dairy cattle; the district was famous for its cheeses. But even then, he found it very hard not to lose money.

Jean finally moved to Ellisland in January 1789. She was pregnant again; the baby, a boy named after Scotland's national hero,[3] was born that summer. He was swiftly followed by three more brothers and a sister (see overleaf).

3. *William Wallace (d. 1305).*

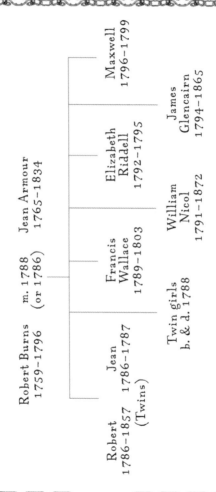

Children of Robert Burns and Jean Armour

Robert Burns 1759–1796   m. 1788 (or 1786)   Jean Armour 1765–1834

Robert 1786–1857   Jean 1786–1787 (Twins)

Twin girls b. & d. 1788

Francis Wallace 1789–1803

William Nicol 1791–1872

Elizabeth Riddell 1792–1795

James Glencairn 1794–1865

Maxwell 1796–1799

Robert Burns's other children

Elizabeth 'Bess' (1785–1816), daughter of Mossgiel servant Elizabeth Paton.

Probably a premature baby (b. & d. 1786), child of dairymaid Mary Campbell ('Highland Mary').

Accused of fathering a child (b. 1787) by Edinburgh servant Meg Cameron.

Robert (b. 1788), son of 'Clarinda's' servant, Jenny Clow, in Edinburgh.

Elizabeth 'Betty' (b. 1791), daughter of Dumfries barmaid Ann Park (though it has sometimes been claimed that Betty was not Burns's child).

In praise of Jean

Of a' the airts the wind can blaw
  I dearly like the west,
For there the bonie lassie lives,
  The lassie I lo'e best.
There wild woods grow, and rivers row,
  And monie a hill between,
But day and night my fancy's flight
  Is ever wi' my Jean.

I see her in the dewy flowers –
  I see her sweet and fair.
I hear her in the tunefu' birds –
  I hear her charm the air.
There's not a bonie flower that springs
  By fountain, shaw, or green,
There's not a bonie bird that sings,
  But minds me o' my Jean.

'Of A' the Airts', 1790

airts: directions.   *blaw: blow.*   *bonie* [sic]*: pretty.*   *lo'e: love.*
row: roll, flow.   *monie: many.*   *wi': with*

tunefu': tuneful.   *shaw: wood.*   *minds: reminds.*

136

Words and music

Along with Burns's mother, and young Nelly-in-the-cornfield, Jean Armour shared in an ancient tradition. She listened to older singers, memorised their words and music, then passed them on, without writing them down, to amuse herself or others. Many songs she sang were hundreds of years old. Sometimes these songs were a blend of old and new; Burns himself often wrote fresh words for ancient melodies. But now, as Scotland was changing fast – and as Scots was falling out of fashion – there was a real danger that this old country music would be lost, for ever.

Danger ~ poet at work!

Burns describes the close link between words and music in his compositions:

'My way is this: I consider the poetic Sentiment, correspondent to my idea of the Musical expression; then choose my theme; begin one Stanza; when that is composed, which is generally the most difficult part of the business, I walk out, sit down now and then, look out for objects in Nature around me that are in unison or harmony with the cogitations of my fancy and workings of my bosom; humming every now and then the air with the verses I have framed: when I feel my Muse beginning to jade, I retire to the solitary fireside of my study, and there commit my effusions to paper: swinging, at intervals on the hindlegs of my elbow chair by way of calling forth my own critical strictures, as my pen goes.'

A 'Musical Museum'

In Edinburgh, in 1787, Burns had met James Johnson – a man with a musical mission! Trained as an engraver, Johnson had invented a new, cheaper way of printing sheet music. Now he planned to use this technology to preserve Scotland's heritage of traditional songs, by publishing them as *The Scots Musical Museum* (6 volumes, 1787–1803).

Would Burns help him? Yes, eagerly – and for free! Over the next ten years he contributed almost 200 songs, for which he received no money. A few were new compositions, but many were Burns's versions of traditional lyrics, collected from family, friends and singers he met on his travels. On Burns's tour of the Highlands in 1787, he was delighted to learn many Gaelic melodies; on a tour of Galloway, in 1793, he collected the prayer before meals which is now known as the 'Selkirk Grace':

> Some hae meat and canna eat,
>   And some wad eat that want it;
> But we hae meat, and we can eat,
>   Sae let the Lord be thankit.

After Burns's dealings with the 'vampire' publisher Creech, he no longer wished to produce whole books of his own poetry. Instead, he sent new compositions, along with his versions of traditional songs, to publishers such as Edinburgh bookseller George Thomson, who printed *A Select Collection of Original Airs for the Voice* in 1792.

On good form

In spite of Burns's worries about the farm, his time at Ellisland was one of the most poetically productive of his whole career. In just three years, he composed many of his best-loved songs and poems, still well known today. These include 'Auld Lang Syne' (but see page 179), 'John Anderson, My Jo' and – unforgettably – 'Tam O' Shanter'.

Dancing with the Devil

A dramatic recitation of Burns's poem 'Tam O' Shanter' is an essential part of any Burns Night celebration (see pages 172–174). One of Burns's longest compositions, it tells what happens when drunken Tam sees – or thinks he sees – a nightmare company of witches and warlocks dancing in a graveyard one Halloween. Meanwhile, his sullen, jealous, neglected wife waits at home, 'nursing her wrath to keep it warm'.

Burns wrote the poem after persuading the English antiquary Francis Grose (1731–1791) – who was visiting southwest Scotland in search of romantic ruins – to make a drawing of the crumbling walls of the old Kirk at Alloway, close to his boyhood home. He may also have remembered how Alloway people feared that ghosts were haunting the Kirk, after a stray bullock got trapped there one night, moaning and bellowing.

More seriously, one scholar has suggested that the poem's threatening images of devils and hell may have been inspired by Burns's guilt over yet another love affair: in March 1791, 'golden-haired' Dumfries barmaid Ann Park gave birth to Burns's daughter, Betty – and died.

There sat Auld Nick, in shape o' beast:
A tousie tyke, black, grim and large,
To gie them music was his charge:
He screw'd the pipes and gart them skirl,
Till roof and rafters a' did dirl.

[*One 'winsome wench' catches Tam's eye:*]

Her cutty-sark, o' Paisley harn
That while a lassie she had worn,
In longitude tho' sorely scanty,
It was her best, and she was vauntie, –
Ah! little ken'd thy reverend grannie,
That sark she coft for her wee Nannie,
Wi' twa pund Scots, ('twas a' her riches),
Wad ever grac'd a dance of witches!
...

Tam tint his reason a'thegither,
And roars out, 'Weel done, Cutty-sark!'
And in an instant all was dark:

from 'Tam O' Shanter', 1791

*Auld Nick: the Devil.   tousie tyke: huge shaggy dog.   gie: give.
gart: made.   skirl: make a shrill sound.   dirl: spin round.*

*cutty-sark: short undershirt or petticoat.   harn: thread.
longitude: length.   vauntie: proud of it.   ken'd: knew.
coft: purchased.   pund: pounds.*

tint: lost, let go of.   a'thegither: altogether.

Poacher turned gamekeeper?

Like everyone else on the southwest coast of Scotland, Burns may well have drunk smuggled rum or sniffed smuggled tobacco. (He liked taking snuff.) But, late in 1789, he was appointed local Gauger (inspector) by the Excise. At last, he could look forward to some financial security! With a sigh of relief, he made plans to give up Ellisland Farm; he moved with Jean and the children to Dumfries in 1791. Their new home was in a back alley known by the townspeople as the 'Stinking Vennel'. Two years later, they moved to a larger, more comfortable dwelling,[4] with a separate study where Burns could read, or write poetry.

As Gauger, Burns's task was to calculate the excise duty payable on luxuries such as tobacco, silk and spirits – and then collect it. He was also meant to track down smugglers, and arrest them if possible.[5] At first the work

4. *in Mill Street (now Burns Street). It had two bedrooms, a parlour and a study. And Jean had a maid to help her.*
5. *If Burns caught a smuggler, he would be paid a bonus of £50 – a whole year's basic Excise salary. He would also be allowed to keep half the smuggled goods.*

involved an exhausting amount of travel – over 200 miles (320 km) a week, on horseback. But in 1792 Burns was promoted to a post in Dumfries itself, where the Excise were making special efforts to stop tobacco smuggling. In 1794 he was offered further promotion.

Domestic bliss

After Burns's death, Jean described their family life together:

'Burns was not an early riser excepting when he had anything particular to do in the way of his profession [as exciseman]. Even tho' he had dined out, he never lay after nine o'clock. The family breakfasted at nine. If he lay long in bed awake he was always reading. At all meals he had a book beside him on the table. He did his work in the forenoon and was seldom engaged professionally in the evening. He was fond of plain things and hated tarts, pies and puddings. When at home in the evening he employed his time in writing and reading with the children playing around him. Their prattle never distracted him in the least.'

For once, Burns's life seemed settled. He was busy with his job; he was happy with Jean and the children. In any spare moments he was composing verses and collecting traditional words and music to send to publishers Thompson and Johnson.

But from time to time he was haunted by thoughts of past possibilities, and tormented by unhappy memories – in particular, by the death of Highland Mary. In 1789 he had written a sweet, mournful lament:

O Mary! dear departed shade!
Where is thy place of blissful rest?
See'st thou thy lover lowly laid?
Hear'st thou the groans that rend his breast?

from 'To Mary in Heaven', 1789

One last kiss

As well, in December 1791, Burns had heard news of 'Clarinda'. She was planning to sail away from Scotland – for ever! – to rejoin her husband. Burns hurried to Edinburgh for one last sentimental meeting. It was not very successful. But afterwards, he sent Clarinda a parting gift: one of the most memorable love-lyrics ever created ('Ae fond kiss'; see pages 124–125).

World-famous novelist Sir Walter Scott (1771–1832) was particularly moved by the poem's fourth stanza:

> Had we never lov'd sae kindly,
> Had we never lov'd sae blindly,
> Never met – or never parted –
> We had ne'er been broken-hearted.

Scott remarked that 'this contains the essence of a thousand love tales and furthermore that one verse is worth a thousand romances'.

Not funny!

Leaving Ellisland in 1791 also meant moving away from Burns's wealthy neighbours, the Riddells. He was suspiciously close friends with lovely, clever, young Maria Riddell, but perhaps the rumours about them were just envious gossip. Anyway, Burns was still able to visit the Riddell home, to talk and recite – that is, until 'the quarrel', at Christmas 1793 or maybe New Year 1794 (accounts differ).

No-one really knows what happened. But probably, after a drunken dinner, Burns and the other 'gentlemen' played at re-enacting a famous episode from ancient Roman history – the Rape of the Sabine Women.[6] Rowdily, but intending no real harm, they 'raided' the ladies in the drawing room. Their hostess, Maria's sister-in-law, was definitely not amused. And 'peasant' Burns was blamed for his 'natural' uncouthness.

6. This was not a 'rape' in the modern sense of the word – 'abduction' would be a better translation. The Romans, being short of women, kidnapped women from a neighbouring tribe and pressured them into marrying Roman husbands. The Romans and the Sabines eventually made peace and became one nation.

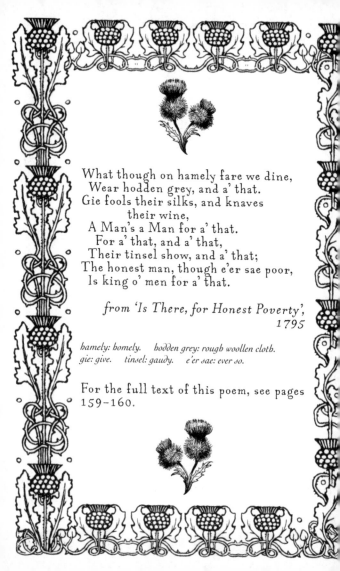

What though on hamely fare we dine,
　Wear hodden grey, and a' that.
Gie fools their silks, and knaves
　　　　their wine,
A Man's a Man for a' that.
　For a' that, and a' that,
　Their tinsel show, and a' that;
The honest man, though e'er sae poor,
　Is king o' men for a' that.

from 'Is There, for Honest Poverty',
1795

hamely: homely.　hodden grey: rough woollen cloth.
gie: give.　tinsel: gaudy.　e'er sae: ever so.

For the full text of this poem, see pages 159–160.

CHAPTER NINE

'A MAN'S A MAN'

We are told that Burns's 'national pride, fierce egalitarianism, and quick wit have become synonymous with the Scottish character itself'.[1] Well, that's as may be. Perhaps, while patting ourselves on the back, we Scots might also, in due modesty, bear in mind one of the Bard's most famous couplets:

> O wad some Pow'r the giftie gie us
> To see oursels as ithers see us!

'To a Louse', 1786

1. *Burns Museum website, 2011: http://www.burnsmuseum.org.uk/*

It is certainly true, however, that Burns's poems and songs are full of passionate 'prejudice' (his word) towards his homeland, along with deep respect for Scotland's ordinary, powerless people. And, for himself, in spite of all his troubles, the Bard never lost his 'lust for individual freedom'.[2]

Burns loved to celebrate this freedom – the more wildly, the better:

> A fig for those by Law protected,
>   Liberty's a glorious feast!
> Courts for cowards were erected,
>   Churches built to please the priest.

'Love and Liberty', 1795

However, Burns lived in what can only be called uncomfortably 'interesting times' (see pages 152–158). As freedom-loving fellow-Scots were increasingly threatened with death or transportation, Burns found it prudent to stay on (just) the right side of the law for the sake of his wife and children. From now on he could not afford to offend rich book-buying patrons, or the British government's Excise

2. *Andro Linklater in* The Spectator, *2009.*

Board. So he compromised, writing ostensibly
'patriotic' verses – but with clever double
meanings. Can we blame him?

> The wretch that would a tyrant own,
>   And the wretch, his true-born brother,
> Who would set the mob above the throne,
>   May they be damned together!
> Who will not sing God Save the King
>   Shall hang as high's the steeple;
> But while we sing God Save the King,
>   We'll ne'er forget the People!

*'Does Haughty Gaul
Invasion Threaten?', 1795*

own: acknowledge (i.e. accept as a legitimate ruler)   Gaul: France.

In fact, Burns had always believed in the
brotherhood of man:

> But ye whom social pleasure charms,
> Whose hearts the tide of kindness warms,
> Who hold your being on the terms,
>   'Each aid to others',
> Come to my bowl, come to my arms,
>   My friends, my brothers!

'Epistle to J. Lapraik', 1785

'Come, ye sons of Liberty'

Burns and the radicals: A timeline

1770s–1780s Radical politicians, writers and thinkers call for reform of British Parliament.

1776–1783 American Revolution: colonies rebel against British rule. Burns admires them:

> But come, ye sons of Liberty,
> Columbia's offspring, brave and free...

Ode for General Washington's Birthday, 1794

Columbia: America.

1787 Burns recalls that 'The story of [William] Wallace poured a Scottish prejudice in my veins which will boil alang there till the flood-gates of life shut in eternal rest.'

1787 After visiting the ruins of the royal castle at Stirling, Burns calls the Hanoverian kings of Britain 'an idiot race to honour lost'. This is dangerously close to treason.

1789 French Revolution begins: French mob overthrows king and queen; later, calls for 'liberty, equality, brotherhood'.

1790 British parliamentarian Edmund Burke condemns mob rule and defends the system of constitutional monarchy in *Reflections on the Revolution in France*.

1790 Feminist Mary Wollstonecraft supports republican, anti-monarchy ideals in *Vindication of the Rights of Men*. Burns later writes a witty, ironic poem, 'The Rights of Women', recited by a well-known actress at Dumfries in 1792.

1791 Burns condemns Scots political leaders who negotiated the Union of Scottish and English parliaments way back in 1707, in return for economic advantages:

> Fareweel to a' our Scottish fame,
>   Fareweel our ancient glory!
> Fareweel ev'n to the Scottish name
>   Sae famed in martial story!
> ...
>
> What force or guile could not subdue
>   Thro many warlike ages
> Is wrought now by a coward few
>   For hireling traitor's wages.
> The English steel we could disdain,
>   Secure in valour's station:
> But English gold has been our bane –
>   Such a parcel of rogues in a nation!

'Fareweel to A' our Scottish Fame', 1791

1792 (January) Revolutionaries in France execute King Louis XVI.

1792 (February) Burns and Excise colleagues sieze a smugglers' ship, the *Rosamund*. In April, Burns purchases four confiscated carronades[3] from the ship – and sends them as a gift to Revolutionary armies in France.

1792 (May) In *The Rights of Man*, English radical Thomas Paine says the right to rule belongs to the people. He is accused of seditious libel and escapes to France.

1792 Controversy when 'Here's a Health' is published in the *Edinburgh Gazette*. Is it Jacobite? Is it harmlessly historical, or an attack on the British government? Burns admits writing the words, but says he did not send them for publication.

Here's a health to them that's awa,
Here's a health to them that's awa,
Here's a health to Charlie, the chief o' the clan,
Altho' that his band be sma'!

3. *These small cannon were the very latest military technology, made in Scotland at the pioneering Carron foundry near Falkirk. In 1787 Burns tried to visit the foundry, was refused admittance, and scratched a poem on the window of a nearby inn, comparing the foundry gates to the gates of Hell.*

May Liberty meet wi' success!
May Prudence protect her frae evil!
May tyrants and tyranny tine i' the mist,
And wander their way to the devil!...

Charlie: Bonnie Prince Charlie (Prince Charles Edward Stuart), leader of the 1745 Jacobite rebellion.   tine: be lost.

1792 (June) 'King's Birthday Riots' in Edinburgh; protesters call for political reform. They burn effigies of the Home Secretary, and plant 'Trees of Liberty'. This song is popular; probably, it's by Burns:

Heard ye o' the tree o' France,
    I watna what's the name o't;
Around it a' the patriots dance,
    Weel Europe kens the fame o't!
...

Fair Freedom, standing by the tree,
    Her sons did loudly ca', man;
She sang a sang o' liberty,
    Which pleased them ane and a', man
...

Let Britain boast her hardy oak,
    Her poplar and her pine, man
...

But seek the forest round and round,
    And soon 'twill be agreed, man,
That sic a tree can not be found
    'Twixt London and the Tweed, man.

watna: don't know.   kens: knows.   sic: such.

155

1792 Radicals in Britain wear 'liberty caps' and sing 'Ça ira' ('It will come'), the song of revolutionary France.

1792 British government arrests members of pro-democracy 'radical societies', bans their meetings, intercepts their mail, sends agents to disrupt their protests, etc.

1792 (July) Several 'reform societies' unite in Edinburgh to form 'Friends of the People'.

1792 Burns writes his mocking song 'The Deil's awa wi' the Exciseman', and protest poem 'The Slave's Lament'.

1792–1793 Radical societies call three 'Conventions [conferences] of the People' in Edinburgh.

1792 (October) Revolutionaries in France execute Queen Marie Antoinette. Later (1795) Burns will write:

'What is there [wrong] in the delivering over a perjured Blockhead and an unprincipled Prostitute to the hands of the hangman...?'

1792 (October) The audience at Dumfries Theatre Royal sings 'Ça ira.' Accused of joining in, Burns says he never 'opened his lips'.

1792 Burns is accused of disloyalty by the Excise Board. He declares that he is attached to the British constitution, 'next after my God'. He is warned to keep quiet and obey orders, or else he will lose his job.

1793 (January) French revolutionary leaders declare war on Britain.

1793 (February) Scottish Convention leader Thomas Muir is convicted and transported to Botany Bay, Australia.

1793–1794 'Reign of Terror' in France; revolutionaries guillotine up to 40,000 'enemies of the people'.

1793 Burns writes his 'freedom song' 'Scots Wha Hae' (see pages 57–58). It is published anonymously, to coincide with the trial of Thomas Muir.

1795 (January) Burns writes his famous song of equality and brotherhood, 'Is There, for Honest Poverty' (see opposite).

1795 To demonstrate his loyalty to the British government, Burns joins the Dumfries Volunteers (a kind of 'home guard' to defend Britain against France). He is too poor to pay for the uniform.

1795 Burns writes his song 'The Dumfries Volunteers'. It ends with the rousing lines:

> We'll ne'er permit a foreign foe
> On British ground to rally!

1796 (February–March) The war with France and bad weather lead to food shortages in many parts of Scotland; in Dumfries there are riots against the British government.

1796 Shortly before he dies, Burns is reported as saying that he is still 'a staunch republican'.

A man's a man

Is there, for honest Poverty
  That hings his head, and a' that;
The coward-slave, we pass him by,
  We dare be poor for a' that!
    For a' that, and a' that,
    Our toils obscure, and a' that,
The rank is but the guinea's stamp,
  The Man's the gowd for a' that.

What though on hamely fare we dine,
  Wear hodden grey, and a' that.
Gie fools their silks, and knaves their wine,
  A Man's a Man for a' that.
    For a' that, and a' that,
    Their tinsel show, and a' that;
The honest man, though e'er sae poor,
  Is king o' men for a' that.

Ye see yon birkie ca'd a lord,
  Wha struts, and stares, and a' that,
Though hundreds worship at his word,
  He's but a coof for a' that.
    For a' that, and a' that,
    His ribband, star and a' that,
The man of independent mind,
  He looks and laughs at a' that.

hings: hangs.   a': all.   gowd: gold.

hamely: homely.   hodden grey: rough woollen cloth.   gie: give.
tinsel: gaudy.   e'er sae: ever so.

birkie: conceited person (as in 'What a birk!').   coof: fool and knave.

A prince can mak a belted knight,
　A marquis, duke, and a' that;
But an honest man's aboon his might,
　Gude faith he mauna fa' that!
　　For a' that, and a' that,
　　Their dignities, and a' that,
The pith o' Sense, and pride o' Worth,
　Are higher rank than a' that.

Then let us pray that come it may,
　As come it will for a' that,
That Sense and Worth, o'er a' the earth
　Shall bear the gree, and a' that.
　　For a' that, and a' that,
　　It's comin yet for a' that,
That Man to Man the warld o'er,
　Shall brithers be for a' that.

'Is There, for Honest Poverty', 1795

mak: make.　aboon: above.　mauna fa': must not fault (deny).

bear the gree: take first place (degree).　brithers: brothers.

A vexed question

As we saw on page 93, in 1786 Burns was ready to leave Scotland for a new life – on a slave plantation in the Caribbean.

We gasp. We puzzle. But the question cannot be avoided. How could 'a friend of Liberty' even think of sailing halfway round the world to exploit fellow human beings, who were so much more oppressed than he would ever be?

The answer is not pretty, but it's realistic. All his life, Burns had lived with the fear of hunger and eviction. He'd seen old men and women shivering in rags and sleeping in ditches. He'd seen smelly, lousy, disease-ridden beggars. He was young and hopeful. He wanted better.

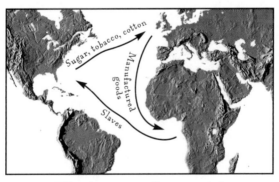

The 'triangular trade'
across the Atlantic

Needs must...

Burns never lost his radical sympathies. But he had a growing family to feed (Elizabeth, born November 1792; James Glencairn, born August 1794; by late 1795, Jean Armour was pregnant again.) In the new house at Mill Street, Dumfries, he employed a servant; he bought a fashionable dress or two for Jean. Burns was proud to see her in nice clothes; she was one of the first women in Dumfries to wear expensive gingham cotton.

But all this needed to be paid for. Burns must earn more money. He must show loyalty! He must prove his worth! He must work harder! And he must secure an Excise pension to support Jean and the children, if – when – he should die!

Whatever people thought of his political views, Burns was clearly intelligent, diligent, capable, and popular with the people of Dumfries. The Excise Board took a chance: late in 1794, they appointed Burns acting supervisor. He threw himself into the task, working 12 hours or more every day, and, although 1794/5 was an exceptionally bitter winter, he continued to patrol his excise district through wind, rain – and snowdrifts.

Even the fittest, strongest man might be weakened by such efforts. But Burns already knew that his own health was failing. Throughout 1794 he had attacks of the depressive illness that had troubled him since childhood. His mental anguish grew worse after his two-year-old daughter, Elizabeth, died in September 1795. So did his physical suffering:

'[I] had scarcely begun to recover from that shock [Elizabeth's death], when I became myself the victim of a most severe rheumatic fever ...after many weeks of a sick bed...I am beginning to crawl across my room, and once indeed have been before my own door in the street.'

Burns, writing at the end of January 1796

Heartsick

Rheumatic fever is an illness that usually starts before the age of 15. Almost certainly, Burns suffered his first attack in childhood. The symptoms are nasty – and frightening: fever, chills, weakness, shortage of breath, and red, swollen, painful joints that make movement excruciating. There may be long-term damage to the heart and sometimes to other organs.

Rheumatic fever occurs following an infection by bacteria. (Typically, these cause sore throats; rheumatic fever is thought to be caused by an immune response to the infection.) Today, it is rare in wealthy developed countries; it is prevented or controlled by antibiotics. But until around 1960, it was a major cause of death among young children. And, as Burns knew painfully well, it can recur over many years, or even for a whole lifetime. Burns may have had attacks when he went to Irvine (see page 80), when he travelled to Edinburgh (see page 112), and at other times during his adulthood.

Hearts weakened by rheumatic fever may fail to pump blood properly; their damaged tissue is also susceptible to infection, called bacterial endocarditis. This can be triggered by anything that causes bacteria to leak into the bloodstream. (Burns complained bitterly of an infected tooth in 1795 – and wrote a poem about it.) Endocarditis is a serious disease; in the past it was often fatal.

The heavy hand...

Although Burns had recovered sufficiently to leave his bed by late January 1796, he was still a very sick man. He complained of 'stiffening joints' – which he thought were a sign of approaching old age (he was 37). But by April he felt 'the heavy hand of SICKNESS' again. In constant pain – and hectically troubled by money worries (because he could not work, his Excise salary had been cut by about 30%) – he decided to follow the advice of Dumfries physician (and friend, and fellow-radical), Dr Maxwell.[4] He must take long horse rides in the fresh air, and go bathing in the sea. It was the latest, most fashionable cure.

In spring and summer, the waters around the coast of Scotland are at their coldest.[5] Yet Brurns braved them. On 3 July 1796 he travelled to Brow Well on the shores of the Solway Firth, about 10 miles (16 km) from Dumfries. On doctor's orders, every day he waded out to stand chest-deep in cold water.

4. *He diagnosed Burns (incorrectly) as suffering from 'flying [acute] gout'.*
5. *They are warmest in September.*

Two weeks later, on 18 July, Burns returned home – so much worse that he could hardly stagger from the horse-drawn cart into his house, where he collapsed.

Jean sent the children to stay with neighbours, so that the noise of their play would not disturb their dying father. Grieving friends called to see him, and he wrote one last letter, to his old enemy, Jean Armour's father, begging him to look after her. By 21 July Burns was delirious; the end could not be far away. Hurriedly, his children were brought home to say a last goodbye.

> The social, friendly honest man,
>   Whate'er he be,
> 'Tis he fulfils great Nature's plan,
>   And none but he.

'Second Epistle to J. Lapraik', 1785

Robert Burns, aged 37, was buried on 25 July 1796, four days after he died. A vast crowd – some say 10,000 men, women and children – lined the streets of Dumfries, while local musicians played – no, not a solemn dirge on the Scottish bagpipes, but London classical music: the Dead March from Handel's oratorio *Saul*. And, in spite of Burns's own republican, revolutionary dying wishes, the loyal Dumfries Volunteers fired a volley of shots over his grave.

And Jean? Bonnie Jean? Burns's faithful, forgiving friend and (probably) the love of his life? As her husband was lowered into his grave she gave birth to their ninth child, a son.[6] Burns's rich friends in Edinburgh started a fund to support her, and commissioned Dr James Currie to write a biography, which would be sold to earn extra money.

6. Jean named the baby Maxwell, after the friendly doctor who had tried to help Burns – but whose tragically misinformed advice had helped to kill him. Jean did not know this, of course.

Dust to dust

Burns's fame grew fast after his death. By 1813, his admirers decided that they must erect a grand monument to his memory. They planned a mausoleum, and, in 1815 they got permission to open the obscure grave where Burns had first been buried, to move his body to this grander resting place.

As workmen lifted the coffin, its cheap wooden planks parted:

'There were the remains of the great poet, to all appearance nearly entire...the lordly forehead, arched and high – the scalp still covered with hair...some of the workmen stood bare-[headed]...their frames thrilling...as they gazed on the ashes of him whose fame is as wide as the world itself....But the effect was momentary...the head seaparated from the trunk and the whole body with the exception of the bones crumbled to dust.'

Quoted in William McDowall,
History of Dumfries, 1867*

*For a fuller text, see:
http://www.dumfriesmuseum.demon.co.uk/frames.html

IN CONCLUSION

Great Scot!

In 2009, Robert Burns narrowly defeated William Wallace in a poll taken by STV (Scottish Television) to identify the world's top Scotsman. Cynics might suggest that this was one mythologised creation contesting another. We have very little reliable information about 'Braveheart' Wallace, and there is still much that remains unknown and perhaps unknowable about Scotland's Bard.

This has not, however, stopped Scots – and others – from creating their own Robert Burnses, very much in their own images.

From the moment Burns died his 'immortal memory' has been romanticised, sanitised, radicalised, nationalised and otherwise transformed to meet the needs of each era. Thus, in 1786, when Burns's poems first appeared in print (and when 'pastoral' was all the fashion), reviewers praised his 'simple and excellent' words which, according to *The Times Literary Characteristical Catalogue*, 'seemed to have flowed without effort from the native feelings of his heart'. In contrast, today we read that Burns was:

- 'an ecumenical poet' (Gerard Carruthers in *The Catholic Herald*, 2009)

- 'the radical poet' (Jock Morris in *Socialist Worker*, 2009)

- 'in love with his own developing writerliness' (Robert Crawford, quoted by Frances Wilson in *The Times*, 2009)

- 'rakish, bookish and blokish' (quoted by Jonathan Gibbs in a review of Robert Crawford's highly praised biography *The Bard*, in the *Financial Times*, 2009).

While he lived, Burns complained that his neighbours did not really understand poetry: they had 'as much idea of a rhinoceros'. It is extraordinary to learn that one of Burns's closest, most intelligent friends considered that 'poetical talent…was not his forte'.[1]

Looking back, Burns himself feared that novelty value plus the 'honest, national prejudice of Scotchmen' might have raised him to 'a height altogether untenable to my abilities'.

That was then – what of now? What might Burns have made of more modern expropriations of his talent: the serious academic studies and controversies, the clubs and societies, the songs (rendered in all kinds of languages, all sorts of musical styles), the tours and tourists, the drunken, pawky recitations, the international fellowships and prizes, the imitators, the apologists, the Scottish national Burns Day (or Burns Night) – and, of course, the ritual of Burns Suppers?

1. *Maria Riddell, 1796; quoted in Donald A. Low (ed.),* Robert Burns: The Critical Heritage *(1974). Instead, Maria considered that Burns excelled in: 'the charms — the sorcery, I would almost call it, of fascinating conversation…nor was any man, I believe, ever gifted with a larger portion of the "vivida vis animi"' [lively force of mind].*

How to hold a Burns Supper

1. Get the date right! The first Burns Supper was mistakenly held on 29 January 1802 (at Greenock). Burns's birthday was 25 January.

2. It's a special occasion, so dress your best. If you've got a tartan, flaunt it!

3. The Host – or, if you're feeling Gaelic, the *Fear an Tighe* (Father of the House) – should greet guests. When all are at table, give thanks for the food. The Selkirk Grace (see page 139) is usual.

4. A first course may be served. Traditionally this is thick soup; sometimes even cock a' leekie (chicken, leeks – and prunes!). But be warned: haggis, followed by cloutie dumpling (the traditional dessert: dried-fruit pudding boiled in a floured cloth), does not lie lightly on the stomach.

5. EEEEW – WAAAAH! What's that? Time to stand up and show respect to THE HAGGIS! A piper, playing proudly, will lead the way, followed by a strong man or boy carrying a large, very hot (and slippery) haggis on a flat platter. Not as easy as it looks. The chef follows, clasping a sharp knife.

6. Toast the haggis. Make sure that there is whisky in your glass (pour some for the

piper and chef, too, and for the haggis-bearer if he is old enough).

7. Address the haggis. No, not for the post, but by reciting Burns's lines 'Fair fa' your honest, sonsie face...' (see pages 175–176). Fit actions to the words, slashing the haggis open with a dramatic (but safe) gesture at: 'trenching your gushing entrails bright'.

8. After that, enjoy your meal. Nowadays, many people prefer vegetarian haggis: it doesn't have entrails, or 'pores' or 'hurdies' (read the poem). The chef often slips this into the room rather surreptitiously, after the old-style meaty one.

9. Now, are you sitting comfortably? Then let the speeches begin! First, the Host will toast the Bard's 'Immortal Memory'. His speech can be about anything he chooses, so long as it's linked to Burns's life, and his place in Scottish culture.

10. Now it's time to hear some of the Bard's own words. Depending on their memories, histrionic talents, or media skills, guests entertain the company with renditions of Burns's poems. However well or badly performed, the highlight is always 'Tam O' Shanter'.

11. Now the Host – or another senior man – takes centre stage, with the Toast to the Lasses. This can be as chaste or as profane

as the assembled company thinks proper. But some speakers find themselves moved to emulate Burns's less delicate sentiments and vocabulary.

12. For maybe the only time in the evening, it's a woman's turn to speak. It's her task to reply on behalf of the Lasses. Like some of Burns's barmaid friends, she may be outspoken and unblushing. Or terribly refined, like Clarinda.

13. If you've been sitting quietly, hoping not to be noticed, then now's the time to feel really, really frightened. Soon it will be your turn to perform a 'party piece'. Not to join in goes against the convivial spirit of the occasion. But – thankfully to many – these old rules are increasingly ignored, or forgotten.

14. By now, most guests will have consumed a fair amount of 'good auld Scotch drink'. And it's time to say goodbye. Will everyone – anyone? – cross and shake hands the right way round, or remember the words to 'Auld Lang Syne?' Probably not. But it doesn't matter...

A good time has been had by all!

Address to a Haggis

Fair fa' your honest, sonsie face,
Great chieftain of the puddin-race!
Aboon them a' ye tak your place,
   Painch, tripe, or thairm:
Weel are ye wordy of a grace
   As lang's my arm.

The groaning trencher there ye fill,
Your hurdies like a distant hill,
Your pin wad help to mend a mill
   In time of need,
While thro' your pores the dews distil
   Like amber bead.

…

Ye Pow'rs, wha mak mankind your care,
And dish them out their bill o' fare,
Auld Scotland wants nae skinking ware
   That jaups in luggies;
But, if ye wish her gratefu' prayer
   Gie her a Haggis!

1786

*Fair fa': good luck to.   sonsie: pleasant, attractive.   aboon: above.
painch: paunch (stomach).   tripe: stomach lining (cooked as food).
thairm: gut.   wordy: worthy.*

*trencher: big plate or dish.   hurdies: buttocks.   pin: skewer.
wad: would.*

*wha mak: who make.   skinking ware: watery food.
jaups: splashes.   luggies: ears*

What would Burns think of such a party? Or of the flash mob that gathered in Edinburgh to shout 'A man's a man for a' that', or the Jean Armour jigsaw puzzle, or the website devoted to 'the finest Robert Burns merchandise, sourced in Scotland, especially for you?'

What would he make of the Burns Picnic on top of Africa's Mount Kilimanjaro? Or the Chinese revolutionaries who chanted his words as they marched along? Would he appreciate being pictured on stamps from Soviet Russia (1956), or – latest news – being given 'a whole new image',[2] as scientists reconstruct his 'real' face from the plaster cast of his skull?

Would he like to learn how his books were sent to cheer Caribbean schoolchildren after an earthquake, or approve of being commodified, as Scotland's top money-making 'cultural asset'?[3]

We don't know. But one thing we can say. Like the work of any great writer, Burns's

2. See The Scotsman, 13 August 2011.
3. 'The legacy of our foremost poet …[carries] tremendous value' – First Minister Alex Salmond, 2009.

poetry changes the way we see the world. Can we look at a mouse, a rose, grand Scottish scenery, or a humble haggis, without his words echoing, however faintly, in our hearts and minds?

Burns turns of phrase

Here are just a few of the phrases whose popularity we owe to Robert Burns:

Best-laid plans
Of mice and men
City gent
Death in the cup
Red, red rose
Parcel of rogues

One last kiss
Love and liberty
As others see us
Cement the quarrel
A strapping youth
The awkward squad

And, with special resonance for the Scots:

My heart's in the Highlands
Charlie is My Darling
Guid auld Scots drink

Cutty Sark
Holy Willie
Unco' good

'Let's sing our sang...'

Sometimes, amid the merriment and marketing, it's hard to remember that Robert Burns was a real human being who lived and breathed, and worked and worried, and died tragically young from a disease that would not have killed him today. His story is romantic in the extreme, but while we smile or shake our heads at his 'fornications' it's all too easy to forget that Robert loved words and the world around him almost as much as he loved women. However muddy, rain-soaked and exhausted, he was moved by the grandeur and pathos of nature. His delight in language, rhyme and rhythm (and in what he could create with them) still shines from the page.

For over 200 years we have admired not only Burns's surprising talent at putting our inner feelings into words, but also his shameless wit, his honesty, his recklessness, his determination and hard work, his defiant bid to escape poverty, his refusal to give in. That is why, even in an age awash with instant celebrities, this flawed, original and, above all, contradictory character is still Scotland's favourite son.

'What an antithetical mind! – tenderness, roughness – delicacy, coarseness – sentiment, sensuality – soaring and grovelling, dirt and deity – all mixed up in one compound of inspired clay!'

Poet George Gordon, Lord Byron (1788–1824)

for auld acquaintance

Why have we not quoted Burns's most celebrated song? The one sung at midnight, every New Year, and at the turning of the Millennium? The one we hum along with but (mostly) don't know the words to?

Well, because, like many of the traditional songs that Burns so lovingly collected, he did not write all the words. The following lines, in a letter from Burns to his friend Mrs Agnes Dunlop, suggest that much of the text of 'Auld Lang Syne' did not originate with him:

'Light be the turf on the breast of the heaven-inspired poet who composed this glorious fragment! There is more of the fire of native genius in it than in half a dozen of modern English Bacchanalians.'

But without Burns to save, augment, polish and preserve this 'fragment' for Scotland and posterity, we would probably not have 'Auld Lang Syne' at all. So, as we remember Auld Aquaintance, let's also honour Burns's 'immortal memory':

The Bard!

Glossary

antiquary A person who is interested in objects or writings from the past, but is not necessarily a systematic historian.

arable farming Growing crops in fields, usually for food.

bard A poet, especially one who is thought of as heroic, or as embodying the spirit of a nation.

commonplace book A miscellaneous collection of poetry, prose quotations and other material of interest, copied out by hand. Often the compiler adds their own notes and comments.

constitutional monarchy A system of government headed by a king or queen whose powers are strictly controlled by parliament and the law.

cottar (Scots) A cottager; a poor tenant, often without land.

crack (Scots and Irish) Conversation; companionable chatter.

crop rotation The practice of sowing different crops in different years, and/or leaving land fallow for a time. It is designed to limit pests and diseases and improve soil fertility.

dominie (Scots) A schoolmaster.

dour (mainly Scots) Grim, miserable, surly.

dreich (Scots) Cold, wet, dark (of weather).

dyke A wall, especially one built to mark a field boundary or to prevent flooding.

Excise Payment collected by a government on foreign goods imported into a country.

GLOSSARY

fallow Uncultivated; left free of crops to rest the soil.

Freemasons An ancient international society, for men only, based on 'brotherly love, faith and charity'. In the 18th century, belonging was a sign of acceptance in 'respectable' society.

gauger An inspector working for the Excise service. (*Gauging* is a technique for calculating the volume of a barrel, so that tax can be charged on the contents.)

habbie An ancient Scottish poetic form often used by Burns; see page 116 note 3.

inbye (Scots) Better-quality farmland, close to village houses.

Jacobite A supporter of the exiled Scottish royal Stuart dynasty. In the 18th century, the Stuarts claimed the right to rule Britain. Their supporters organised several rebellions, most importantly in 1715 and 1745. Robert Burns's grandfather sympathised with them.

Kirk The Protestant Presbyterian Church of Scotland. ('Presbyterian' means governed by local church leaders, not by bishops or other religious leaders.)

loch Lake (a Gaelic word).

makar (Scots) A national poet.

mausoleum A grand building designed as a resting place for the dead.

Muses According to the ancient Greeks and Romans, these nine goddesses inspired all the arts – poetry, music, dance, etc. The word can also be used to describe any woman by whom an artist claims to be inspired.

nymph A young goddess or nature spirit; also a poetic term for a young woman, especially in pastoral verse.

  181

Old and New Lichts (Scots) Rival groups within the Kirk. Old Lichts (Lights) believed in strict rules and punishments; New Lichts were more moderate.

outbye (Scots) Poor-quality farmland, often on the outskirts of a village, mostly used for grazing.

pastoral A style of verse describing life in an idealised, imaginary countryside.

pawky (Scots) Sly, archly knowing.

primsie (Scots) Easily shocked.

radical Holding views that call for major social or political change; literally, 'from the roots'.

republican Advocating government by elected leader(s), not by a king or other hereditary ruler.

rig (Scots and northern English) A ridge of earth in a field; a typical feature of Scottish farmland.

stackyard A yard where stacks of corn waiting to be threshed, and sometimes hay (dried grass used as fodder for animals), were stored in safety.

suffragettes People who, in the early 20th century, used direct action and sometimes violence to campaign for votes for women.

swain A young countryman or lover, in pastoral verse.

tenant farmer A man or woman who rents a farm, usually from a richer, more powerful person or company.

tinder Very dry material (such as wood shavings) that burns easily; used to light fires.

transportation A punishment used in the 18th and 19th centuries for convicted criminals: they were shipped to distant, dangerous lands, such as Australia, sometimes for life.

A Burns timeline

1759 Robert Burns (RB) born 25 January in Alloway.

1765 RB and brother Gilbert are sent to school at Alloway Mill. After the teacher leaves, local families hire their own teacher, John Murdoch.

1766 Burnes family moves to Mount Oliphant Farm.

1766–1770 Young RB learns many traditional stories and songs from old servant Betty Davidson.

1772 RB sent to Parish School at Dalrymple to improve his handwriting.

1773 Studies English, French, Latin with former teacher John Murdoch, at Ayr.

1774 RB writes first song, in praise of harvest-worker Nellie Kirkpatrick: 'Once I Lov'd a Bonnie Lass.'

1775 RB continues to compose poems as he works on his father's farm.

1776 RB sent by father to Kirkoswald to study geometry, land-measuring and surveying.

1777 The farm at Mount Oliphant fails. Burnes and his family move to Lochlie Farm, near Tarbolton.

1779 RB goes to country-dancing classes at Tarbolton, against his father's wishes.

1780 RB forms Bachelor's Club in Tarbolton, to debate current affairs and philosophy. Falls in love with young housekeeper Alison Begbie, and writes letters proposing marriage to her. She rejects him.

1781 RB becomes a Freemason. Moves to Irvine to learn how to dress (process) flax.

1782 **1 January:** Flax-dressing workshop burns down. RB becomes friends with sailor Richard Brown, who admires his songs. RB reads *Scottish Poems* by tragic young Edinburgh poet Robert Fergusson (1750–1774). RB returns to Lochlie. His father is unwell and preoccupied by legal dispute with landlord.

1783 RB begins to write a commonplace book. RB and Gilbert plan to rent farm at Mossgiel, helped by liberal-minded local lawyer Gavin Hamilton.

1784 RB's father William Burnes dies, aged 63. RB, his mother and his siblings move to Mossgiel Farm, near Mauchline. RB has affair with Elizabeth Paton, his mother's servant.

1785 RB meets Jean Armour. RB's first child, daughter of Elizabeth Paton, is born. RB is forced to admit guilt in local Kirk (church). RB's mother brings up the baby. Harvest fails at Mossgiel farm (because RB bought poor-quality seed, and because of bad weather). RB's younger brother, John, dies. RB writes many of his greatest poems, including satires against the strict 'Old Lichts' of the Kirk. Handwritten copies are circulated among friends and admirers in southwest Scotland. RB sets up 'Club of Fornicators' at Mauchline.

1786 (or late 1785) Jean Armour becomes pregnant. RB gives her a written promise to marry.

1786 Farming at Mossgiel is not going well. RB plans to make new career on a slave-plantation in Jamaica. Before he leaves he plans to publish a book of poems.

April: RB meets 'Highland Mary' (Mary Campbell), a maid at a local big house. She returns to her family in Cowal, Argyll, probably pregnant. RB may plan to take her with him to Jamaica. Jean Armour returns to Mauchline. Leaders of the Kirk accuse her and

RB of fornication. RB goes into hiding.

31 July: RB's first book, *Poems, Chiefly in the
Scottish Dialect*, is published at Kilmarnock. It is a
great success. RB agrees to wait for a later ship,
having been warned that he has chosen a dangerous
route; he sees Jean again, but also writes to
Highland Mary.

1 September: RB is persuaded to delay his
departure by a poetry-loving Kirk minister, who shows
RB's book to Edinburgh poet Thomas Blacklock.

3 September: Jean Armour gives birth to twins,
Robert and Jean. RB's fame spreads. Blacklock
praises his work. RB delays departure again.

20 or 21 October: Highland Mary, and probably
her unborn baby, die at Greenock. RB, informed by
letter, is horrified. Mary's family curse him.

28 November: RB arrives in Edinburgh, hoping to
find fame and fortune.

1787 Second ('Edinburgh') edition of RB's *Poems*
published. Meets leaders of polite society. Is
befriended by rich patrons: Lord Glencairn and Mrs
Frances Anna Dunlop. Freemasons' Grand Lodge of
Scotland proclaims Burns to be 'Caledonia's Bard'.

RB tours the Borders. Is made an honorary
burgess (citizen) of the town of Dumfries. Accused
of fathering a child by Meg Cameron, a servant in
Edinburgh. Tours West Highlands.

Returns to Mauchline and is reconciled with Jean
Armour, then returns to Edinburgh. Tours North and
East Highlands and Stirlingshire.

Meets musician and inventor James Johnson.
Works with him to preserve old songs, and write new

words for ancient tunes. Results published 1787–1803 as *The Scots Musical Museum*.

Meets Agnes ('Nancy') MacLehose; they exchange passionate letters, using the pastoral names 'Clarinda' and 'Sylvander'. At the same time, RB has affair with her servant Jenny Clow.

1788 February: Returns to Mauchline. Says he is 'disgusted' by Jean Armour.

March: Jean Armour gives birth to twin daughters. Both babies soon die.

RB agrees to rent farm at Ellisland, near Dumfries. Kirk leaders and lawyers agree that RB is legally married to Jean Armour.

June: RB Moves to Ellisland. Jean and their children join him 6 months later.

July: RB is commissioned as Excise Officer.

November: Jenny Clow gives birth to RB's son. RB ill with severe throat infection.

1789 August: Jean Armour gives birth to son, Francis Wallace. RB starts work as Excise Officer.

1790 RB turns down offer to write for *Star* newspaper in London, also invitation to apply for post as Professor of Agriculture at Edinburgh University. Barmaid Anna Park gives birth to RB's daughter.

1791 Jean Armour gives birth to son, William Nicol. RB, Jean Armour and family move to Dumfries. RB's songs published in George Thomson's *A Select Collection of Original Scottish Airs for the Voice*.

1792 RB made member of Royal Company of Archers, Edinburgh (monarch's ceremonial bodyguard; a great honour). Jean Armour gives birth to daughter, Elizabeth Riddell. Excise questions RB's loyalty after he shows support for French Revolution.

1793 Burns family moves to better house in Dumfries.

1793–1794 RB tours Galloway collecting songs.

1794 Turns down offer to write for *Morning Chronicle* in London. Jean Armour gives birth to son, James Glencairn. RB made supervisor of Excise at Dumfries.

1795 RB joins Dumfries Volunteers.

1795–1796 Dec.–Jan.: RB very ill (rheumatic fever).

1796 Food riots in Dumfries. RB's pay is reduced because he is too ill to work.

    18 June: RB writes to Jean Armour's father, asking him to look after (very pregnant) Jean.

    3–16 July: RB sent to Brow Well near Dumfries for sea-bathing 'cure'.

    21 July: Dies in Dumfries, aged 37.

    24 July: Lies in state in Dumfries Town House.

    25 July: 10,000 mourners attend RB's funeral; on same day, Jean Armour gives birth to son, Maxwell.

1800 Dr James Currie publishes influential but inaccurate biography of RB.

c.1800 Bawdy songs, written and/or edited by RB, published as *The Merry Muses of Caledonia*.

1801 First celebration of RB's birthday at Burns's Cottage, Alloway (on the wrong day). First recorded Burns Supper, on anniversary of RB's death, at Alloway. Food served includes haggis and a sheep's head. World's first Burns Club founded at Greenock, by merchants from Ayrshire.

1802 First Burns Supper on his actual birthday, at Greenock.

1815 RB's body moved to mausoleum in Dumfries churchyard.

1820–1823 Burns Monument built at Alloway.

1834 Jean Armour dies and is buried beside RB.

1844 Grand festival in RB's honour held in Ayrshire.

1859 Celebrations in many parts of Scotland mark the centenary of RB's birth.

1882 Statue of RB unveiled in Dumfries.

1885 Burns Federation set up, to link hundreds of Burns Clubs worldwide.

1924 Translation of poems makes RB a favourite in Russia.

1937 US novelist John Steinbeck uses line from RB's 'To a Mouse' as a title for his prize-winning novel *Of Mice and Men*.

1951 The same poem inspires another US writer, J. D. Salinger, in *The Catcher in the Rye*.

1956 USSR issues stamp with portrait of RB.

1971 RB portrait decorates Clydesdale Bank £5 note.

1996 Musical *Red Red Rose* celebrates RB's life.

2000 RB's poem 'Is There, for Honest Poverty' sung at first meeting of Scottish Parliament since 1707.

2007 RB appears on Royal Bank of Scotland £5 note.

2008 Bob Dylan chooses RB's 1794 song 'A Red Red Rose' as his 'biggest inspiration'. Musical *Clarinda*, about RB's relationship with Nancy McLehose.

2009 Prince Charles reads RB's poem 'My Heart's in the Highlands' (1789) for BBC website. Royal Mint issues £2 coin with quotation from 'Auld Lang Syne'. RB is voted the Greatest Scot ever.

2010 First Jean Armour Supper held in Glasgow.

2011 New Burns Museum and heritage centre opens in Alloway.

Index

Poems quoted in the text

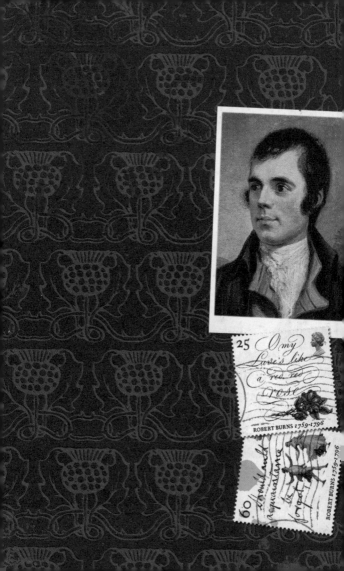